# Red Army Sniper

*Available:*

SNIPERS AT WAR
*An Equipment and Operations History*
John Walter

EASTERN FRONT SNIPER
*The Life of Matthäus Hetzenauer*
Roland Kaltenegger

*Forthcoming:*

THE SNIPER ENCYCLOPAEDIA
*An Illustrated History of World Sniping*
John Walter

LADY DEATH
*The Memoirs of Stalin's Sniper*
Lyudmila Pavlichenko

# Red Army Sniper

## A Memoir of the Eastern Front in World War II

### Yevgeni Nikolaev

*Foreword by*
### Albrecht Wacker

*Translation by*
### David Foreman

Greenhill Books

*Eastern Front Sniper*

This edition published in 2017 by
Greenhill Books,
c/o Pen & Sword Books Ltd,
47 Church Street, Barnsley,
S. Yorkshire, S70 2AS

www.greenhillbooks.com
contact@greenhillbooks.com

ISBN: 978–1–78438–236–0

Translated from *Sniper Duels: Stars on my Rifle,*
(Yauza, Moscow, 2009), a revised and expanded edition of
*Stars on my Rifle* (Leninizdat, Leningrad [St Petersburg], 1985)

CIP data records for this title are available from the British Library

Printed and bound in England by
TJ International Ltd, Padstow, Cornwall

Typeset in 12.1/15 pt Minion Pro

# Contents

Yevgeni Nikolaev, as a decorated veteran in the 1980s.

# Preface

This book is not the work of a writer. The author was a sniper – a role that he came into during the Second World War and never escaped. In the naïve heroism of the narrative we encounter the ageing fighter reflecting on his younger self of forty years ago, seeking to unearth the facts of war and the words to capture his experience.

The biography is thus made up of selective memories, an assemblage of experiences moulded over time that insists on the narrative of a victor. It cannot accommodate ambiguities because it is precisely through these proverbial blind spots that the protagonist gains the ability to locate himself and create a fixed identity within the chaos and impossibility of war. Horror, pain, disarray and catastrophe do not figure in this book. Instead, the text is structured by an unbroken line of heroic acts; of unity between mother and son, soldier and fatherland, comrades in arms, commanders and subordinates, but also between the past and the present. These relationships are what give us a deeper insight into the realities of war combined with an impressive collection of photographs, documents, Soviet newspaper clippings and private correspondence.

With this publication in English, a part of our country's history is unexpectedly crossing borders. Nikolaev's tale gains an entirely new audience and loses the predictability and ordinariness that usually accompany such literature in Russia. It is through this journey of translation that the book gains the status of an original historical document.

The episodes of military action between 1941 and 1945 have been reconstructed by the author significantly later – in time for the fortieth anniversary of Victory Day – and were composed during times of peace, on the eve of *Perestroika* and the sunset of the USSR. Carried across decades, the events detailed in this book introduce the 21st-century reader to a colourful representative of the snipers of the Great Soviet Fatherland; Nikolaev's words offer a complete and authentic experience.

*Dina Nikolaeva*

Granddaughter of
Yevgeni Nikolaev

# Foreword

Yevgeni Nikolaev was a member of the Soviet *Narodnyi Komissariat Vnutrennikh Del* (NKVD – the People's Commissariat of Internal Affairs), who fought on the Leningrad Front in 1941 and 1942. He appears as number 32 on a Russian list of Second World War snipers with the most kills.

Shortly after the collapse of the Soviet Union, Russian historians engaged in critical debate on the country's history for the first time. Archives were opened for research and access was granted to foreign historians with the goal of obtaining an objective perspective on the past. However, this new transparency was short-lived. Vladimir Putin's rise to power meant the closing of archive doors once again and a return to propaganda to restore the image of Russian glory. Till this day, serious historiography remains uncharted territory.

Nikolaev's autobiography is an interesting example of Soviet propaganda literature and the historical misrepresentation it fashions. The text – which was composed around 1980, decades after the events it details, with the help of a journalist – must therefore be read critically. For instance, we are told that Finland attacked the Soviet Union when the truth is that the Soviet Union attacked Poland and Finland to reclaim territory it had held before the First World War.

The NKVD is repeatedly presented as a harmless troop of angelic moral heroes, when in reality, the agency was a Stalinist organisation of ferocious terror directly responsible for the deaths of 3,000,000 Soviet citizens and foreigners. The NKVD was like the German SS: both practised the systematic destruction of anyone deemed an enemy of the state. This includes the Katyn massacre in which the NKVD murdered tens of thousands of Polish soldiers. Moreover, although the secret-service arm of the NKVD, *Smersh*, was notorious for its brutality, the reader encounters virtually no criticism of its activities. It was where Nikolaev served.

The killing of Nazis is glamorised as a sport for 'real men'. Nazis are portrayed as dumb animals walking in a straight line to the slaughterhouse, unaware of their destiny. Idioms like 'exterminators of the Nazi scum' are used as synonyms for the Russian snipers. These propaganda slogans reveal a biographer whose recollections are in perfect alignment with the Stalinist goal of reducing any opponent to an inhuman object.

Although the German snipers facing the Russians were proverbial aces flown in from Berlin and equipped with superior technology like telephone lines to their foxholes, they are nevertheless presented as inferior to the Soviets. Conversely, the Russian NKVD sniper brings down the enemy aircraft by a single shot from his Mosin-Nagant rifle.

This exaggerated patriotism is no less strong when it concerns the author's own actions. In a single ambush, he recollects killing eleven Nazis one after the other, including two colonels and a general who had just arrived from Berlin to inspect the front line. The pathos continues to build as his first action after this event is to inform his beloved mother of how he is fulfilling his duty to his country and family as an obedient son.

The management of truth is in direct relation to the auto-biographical memories, which cast the Russian soldier as the moral hero. This is a man committed to serving his country whatever the cost to his personal comfort or life. According to Nikolaev, Russian snipers went into action without a supply of food or water

– comforts which could distract their attention from their targets. Nikolaev's foxhole was his home amid starvation and dehydration until he could present a host of dead Nazis to his esteemed major.

Eventually Nikolaev is wounded. It should come as no surprise that even this traumatic event is displaced by symptoms of patriotism. Consider the description of how his Russian military presentation watch, which he carries in his trouser pocket, is driven into his stomach by shrapnel, although an explosive rifle bullet also hits his left arm. Nikolaev goes on to save a lieutenant's life before seeking out the medical unit. The triumphant arc is complete once the reader learns that a masterful surgeon is attending to the injured, and that with the help of a skilled watchmaker, who happens to be present, the two successfully remove all the parts of watch and shrapnel from Nikolaev's guts.

Nikolaev's narrative trades in psychological effects, with an incessant ardour that demands both the reader's patience and their critical resistance to its pull. It is a fascinating example of Russian military literature precisely due to its devoted and adamantly patriotic author.

*Albrecht Wacker*

# Red Army Sniper

*Dedicated to the radiant memory of my mother, Anna Lukinichna Nikolaeva, who brought me up to be the man I became and am, and it was only on account of her enormous love for her son that I survived at the front and returned home*

Another war
Another blockade . . .
But perhaps we can forget about them?
I sometimes hear:
'Don't,
Don't aggravate old wounds.
For it's true that we're tired
Of tales of war.
And on the blockade leafed through
Quite enough verse.'

And it may seem
These words
Are true and convincing.
But if that is the truth,
Such truth
Is not true!

Not for nothing am I concerned,
That that war should not be forgotten:
For its memory is our
Conscience.
We need it,
As a source of strength . . .

# From the Author

Inspired and supported by that great wartime writer and poet Konstantin Simonov, I have summoned up the courage to write a book about the war, taking as an epigraph the verses by the Leningrad poet Yuri Voronov, which have become seared into my soul. I have done this not only in order that the war should not be forgotten, but also that my tale might be of benefit to our up and coming generation.

Progressing through the grand school of life and war, as a rank-and-file soldier who travelled the whole way from the Narva Gate in Leningrad to the Brandenburg Gate in Berlin, enduring with his comrades the entire 900 days of the siege, I wish to share with young people my experiences during our homeland's most arduous years, when each of us was put to the test in terms of courage and steadfastness. I wanted through my narrative to open up one more page in the history of the Great War for the Fatherland, to describe how the snipers' movement was born and grew to mass proportions in Leningrad and played a huge role in the positional 'trench warfare' around the besieged city.

The veterans of the war are aging. Almost fifty years have passed since the times described in the book *Stars on my Rifle*. Basically it is about the beginning of the war, the first year – the most difficult year for the besieged city of Leningrad. I began to gather material back in the war years: I looked into the events and the people, noted every characteristic feature of day-to-day wartime life, collected newspaper cuttings and documents, kept photographs and remembered stories told by my comrades. All this came in handy and helped me in working on the manuscript.

I am profoundly grateful to my fellow townsfolk of Tambov, comrades in arms – veterans of the 21st (109th) Rifle Division of the NKVD forces, especially to the former commissar of the 14th Rifle Regiment, the late Reserve Colonel Ivan Ilyich Agashin, who accorded me great help and constant support in the process of writing this book.

The book is into its second edition because the material prepared for publication by Leninizdat underwent intensive 'trimming'. The first version of the manuscript saw the removal of much that could not be mentioned during that period of stagnation, or material that was of no interest to the publishers in terms of the geography of the events. Now the book has been significantly altered and supplemented and errors in the first edition have been corrected.

Nikolaev with his wife Tatyana and
his daughter Olga.

Nikolaev finished the war serving with an artillery
unit and is seen here in the full uniform
of an artillery captain.

# 1.

# Lieutenant Butorin
# Has an Idea

It was mid-September 1941. The sun's heat was surprisingly merciless for this time of year. The snow-white clouds floated lazily from beyond the Pulkovo heights and dissolved somewhere over Leningrad's Morskoy port. Enjoying the silence and glad still to be alive, we sat stretching out our weary legs clad in heavy canvas boots, which were covered with a thick layer of dust. We sat in silence, propped on our elbows in the long green grass, relaxing, idly observing the way our fellow-villagers were working as they strengthened the regiment's defence works and watching the tree tops lazily swaying in Sheremetyev Park,[1] which lay spread out behind our unit's position.

We were ten regimental reconnaissance scouts, who had just returned from yet another mission. Tightly wrapped up in a cape lay the eleventh of our number, who had been killed, and we had carried him back. He was already beyond sharing our delight.

---

1. Sheremetyev Park used to be located close to where Stachki and Marshal Zhukov Avenues now intersect.

I sat away from the group, writhing from the pain in my left hand. 'As long as they don't notice I'm wounded. They'll pack me off to hospital and what hope then of getting back to the unit!' Blood from the wound was already gradually seeping into the palm of my hand, and, with my other hand, I surreptitiously wiped it away with a clump of grass.

A regimental medic happened to be walking past. I decided to call him.

'Would you mind taking a look at my arm, mate. Only don't poke around too much. It's a bit sore.'

'Wow, you're wounded, brother! There's a hole in your sleeve! Where did they get you like that? And how long ago?' asked the medic, in a concerned tone.

'Oh, about twenty minutes, since we got back from reconnaissance.'

'Why did you keep quiet till now?' he asked, opening up his bag. 'We'll bandage it up, put on a tourniquet, and stop the bleeding.'

He zealously bandaged it up, then applied a tourniquet, straight onto the quilted sleeve – squeezed the arm by the left shoulder with a thin, rubber tube.

'And now get yourself off to the regimental dressing station; you've got to get a tetanus injection,' he ordered, closing up his bag.

The blood that had been continuously running into my palm really had stopped flowing, but the arm was still sore.

'Well, thanks for that anyway, old fellow! A pity you can't do anything to help him,' and I nodded in the direction of the dead man wrapped up in canvas.

'Yes . . . in such cases medicine is, as they say, powerless,' he muttered. 'But you should get a move on unless *you* want to end up wrapped up like that.'

It was hard for me to admit that, to some extent, I was responsible for the death of our mate . . . I had been leading the group. The objective of establishing where the enemy were at the moment and who was situated in line with us on the left side had been achieved almost without effort. The enemy were right next to us, in front.

They had already captured Uritsk and had been stopped before the Pulkovo Heights. Our neighbours on the left turned out to be a battalion of the 6th Regiment of our own division. To our right lay the Gulf of Finland.

Having achieved the objective, we almost got into a shooting match on the way with, it turned out, a mounted patrol of our own border guards. We were returning to our regiment in good spirits. We were heading towards Leningrad through territory already in our possession, along a broad concrete highway, now deserted, which was without any doubt visible to the enemy. To be more precise, owing to my inexperience and an excess of zeal, it was only me walking along the highway – as the senior member of the group. I had ordered the troops to go along the deep ditch on the right hand side of the road, which kept them well hidden from view. And also to spread themselves out, 8–10 metres apart. Only the head and shoulders of the tallest in the group, Private Kotelnikov, who was bringing up the rear, rose above the level of the road.

I was walking along the highway because it seemed more convenient; everybody and everything would be visible. And my lone figure could scarcely be of much interest to the enemy. However, it seems I nevertheless drew the attention of the fascists; mortar bombs and shells were suddenly flying in our direction. Falling a long way short, they began exploding in an empty field, getting closer and closer to the road. I instantly gave orders to move at the double, and began running myself, while continuing to watch the explosions of the shells. A minute later it was as if somebody coughed beside me and struck me heavily on the left arm with the flat surface of a plank. Grunting with the pain, I only then sized up what was what and, pressing my right hand on the smitten area, scooted into the ditch. After running another ten metres from the momentum, I stopped. The explosions had ceased by then. I did a visual count of the troops; there were only ten of them with me.

'Where's the eleventh?' I asked, surveying the group. 'Where's Kotelnikov?'

'He was bringing up the rear,' somebody replied.

'I know that. I put him at the tail of the column myself, to keep an eye on all of you. But where is he now? What's happened to him? He can't have been swallowed up by the earth!'

I looked at the bare fields, devoid of a single bush, on both sides of the highway and did not see anybody,

'That's not so good. We'll all have to go back and look for Kotelnikov.' We found him already dead, in the same ditch, 300 metres back.

And now we were home. My arm was still aching, but I didn't hurry to the dressing station; I sat thinking. It was the third month of the war. A few days back we were in Leningrad – the remnants of the 154th NKVD Rifle Regiment. Up until the perfidious fascist attack on our country the regiment – its headquarters, rearguard and some of its detachments – was based in a small border town in Karelia.

The real battle for us began on 26 June 1941, when Finland formally declared war on the Soviet Union in an attempt to regain territory we'd taken during the Winter War of 1939–40. But up till then, from the 22nd onwards, there were small-scale, sporadic clashes with the enemy. In the course of fierce and bloody battles we had to withdraw through Vyborg towards Leningrad. It was not an easy journey for any of us. We lost many troops and officers dead and wounded.

And so several days earlier the survivors of our regiment had been added as reinforcements to the 14th Red Banner Rifle Regiment of the 21st NKVD Rifle Division. The regimental commander was Lieutenant Colonel Rodionov. On the nearby south-western approaches to Leningrad, the Forty-Second Army was in action. It also included our division which consisted of the 6th and 8th Rifle Regiments as well as our own, the 14th. The divisional commander was Colonel Mikhail Panchenko.

The division received orders to defend Leningrad from the south, from the Gulf of Finland to the River Neva and, farther eastward, to Zapevki, and not to let the enemy into the city.

The 14th Regiment, which had only just occupied the defence sector allotted to it by the divisional commander, hastily entrenched itself, digging in furiously. This was the last barrier before Leningrad. It ran directly behind the city of Uritsk, which was only a few kilometres from Leningrad's Kirov district. From our trenches the chimney stacks of the Kirov works were clearly visible in daylight. In the evenings the lights of rockets, which did not go out over the first trench line, were reflected in the windows of the buildings in the suburb of Avtovo. The second echelons of the regiment and the division were located right in Leningrad itself. The defenders of Leningrad lived with one thought in mind: to protect their native city, not allow the enemy into it. To hold out, just to hold out!

All this passed through my mind while I tried to get used to the unremitting pain in my wounded arm. A little to one side of us, a young Komsomol lieutenant was sitting on the parapet, his legs dangling into the trench. He was Vasily Butorin, who had just joined the regiment. He was immediately appointed to command the 5th Company. The lieutenant's sparklingly shined boots gleamed in the rays of the setting sun. A pleasant blond fellow of average height, with broad shoulders and blue eyes, he was built like a circus acrobat. His uniform was perfectly cleaned and pressed; his tunic was tautly stretched by a broad officer's belt – you couldn't have stuck a finger behind it! And at the same time his whole appearance and behaviour bespoke a seasoned, trained officer. And we felt it straight away, especially since the lieutenant's chest bore an iridescent scarlet and gold Order of the Red Banner which was already thoroughly worn. Attached to his belt by long straps, as on a sailor, hung a TT pistol in a black holster. He appeared to be about twenty-five. Now, as he looked at the thinned trees in Sheremetyev Park and listened to the noise of vehicles beyond it, the commander was focussing his thoughts on something. Perhaps he was thinking about his home town of Barnaul, where he had been born and grown up, about his family, about his wife Varvara, who was in the Kalinin Region. Or perhaps, and more likely, he was thinking about the chances of the men in his company carrying out the regimental commander's order: to complete by morning the equipping of the communication routes, dugouts and rifle pits in the trenches. Working their guts out, all his officers and men were moving the armed turrets and steel shields only just delivered from the Kirov works and stringing them out in a line from the park. Harnessed like Volga boatmen, some of the men were dragging over logs which had been stripped of branches and twigs and sawn to the right size to provide covering for the dugouts. They were also dragging timber from houses which had been destroyed in the village of Dachnoye.

Who knows what the lieutenant was thinking about at this moment – but it was evident that he found it painful to look at the trees felled by the war in the once beautiful Sheremetyev Park, with which he was familiar from peacetime. As a skilled officer who had fought in the Winter War with Finland, he knew from experience that logs from freshly felled trees placed crosswise on dugouts in three or four layers would be much sounder than old dry logs. For in fresh timber, even if it is cut up for firewood, a trace of life remains. And if that was so, it had to offer some resistance. It was apparent that the lieutenant was happy with the smart and careful way his troops were laying these logs on the dugouts. He knew how today's 'guts out' effort would pay off tomorrow. By burrowing deeply and soundly into the earth it would be possible to keep the company's personnel alive. And there they would hammer the enemy day and night, in all weathers – 'fight to the death', as the regimental commander had put it yesterday. These words were well understood by every soldier and officer in the company. The necessary commands had been given to them and everyone knew what his responsibilities were. The main thing was not to interfere with the commanders of the platoons and detachments, not to stifle their initiative and to trust one's subordinates. And Lieutenant Butorin did not interfere. He was confident that the men of the company would not let him down. Behind them was Leningrad!

The lieutenant's reflections were interrupted by Regimental Commissar Agashin, who turned up in the company position. The men got up and stood at attention, having spotted their commissar before the company commander did. Having noticed our movement, the lieutenant looked round and, seeing Agashin, leapt easily into a trench and hurried to meet him.

Before the war Ivan Agashin had been a commissar in a district junior officer training school in the frontier forces of the Leningrad military district. An experienced political instructor, he had packed a lot of living into his forty-plus years. Solidly built, thick-set, with an intelligent and determined face, a thick head of hair which had already grown grey at the temples with the stresses of war, Commissar Agashin astounded us with his bubbling energy and a youthful enthusiasm uncharacteristic of his age. Within the regiment they were fond of him; he was modest, laconic, relaxed and fair. What he said was always powerful and convincing. They liked him for his honesty and personal courage, qualities which are particularly valued in a man. The troops were ready at any minute to follow their commissar through fire and water. I liked the way, possibly characteristic of Pskov, in which he pronounced the word *dolzhny* [must] with an extra syllable ('*dolozhny*'). And when he said it, we knew we *really* 'must' – for the Motherland, the Party, and the people, for the sake of our past and future life. Especially now, in times of severe ordeal. That was how we had been brought up from childhood, from the schoolroom.

'Commander of the 5th Company, Lieutenant Butorin!' he crisply reported. 'The company is occupied with fitting out the dugouts. The company includes regimental scouts who have just got back from a mission. They are recovering, as has already been reported to headquarters by telephone. Greetings, Comrade Commissar!'

Saluting, Agashin extended his hand to Butorin. And, having greeted us, the commissar gestured with his hand: 'Sit down, lads!' and said:

'Yes, I know about the results of the mission. Well done, boys. Let them recover. So what are you thinking about, lieutenant?'

'I was just wondering about ... I had an idea, Comrade Commissar.'

'Let's have it, share it with us.'

We scouts listened to the conversation between the officers, wondering what our likeable lieutenant had come up with.

'Comrade Commissar, I was recalling the war against the Finns. The Finnish "cuckoos", their snipers. I was thinking, why not organise a school like that within the regiment? Well, maybe not a school – that's a bit grandiose – but a course like that, for ten or fifteen men initially?' And he looked questioningly at the commissar, who was listening attentively to the lieutenant, apparently weighing something up in his mind.

'While we're standing here in reserve, I undertake to train some top class snipers.'

'What about resources?' asked Agashin. 'What else will be needed apart from men, and your experience and will?'

'Resources? Depends on circumstances! I've already been making inquiries and the regiment has some snipers' rifles. They're just lying there, bathing in oil at the weapons store. Completely new! So that's something!'

'Well, that's a practical idea. I'll report it to the regimental commander today. I'm already sure he'll approve it. In the meantime recruit some "students" for your "academy", lieutenant. You've probably got an idea who.'

'Yes, sir, Comrade Commissar! I've almost assembled a team – just from my company. But,' and the lieutenant nodded in our direction. 'could you let me have some of the scouts? Fellows like that would be good for a start; they're smart and gutsy. Many of them are good at sport.'

'How long will it take to train them? You realise, the situation...'

'We'll make it simple: a bit of theory, the equipment and how to use it. We do the exam right on the front line – with live targets! Even so it's bound to take about fifteen days.'

'Well, that time-frame can be given for a good cause,' said Agashin. Then, as if to bring the conversation to an end, added: 'Well it's settled: we'll let you have Nikolaev from reconnaissance and you can take Dobrik and Semyonov. And take Rakhmatullin from the 8th Company – I've heard he used to be a hunter; he could hit a squirrel in the eye. And Sergeant Karpov from the ammunition platoon would likely be a good choice and . . . well, who else is there – you can let me know later.'

Three days after this noteworthy conversation a group of soldiers, myself included, were holding in their hands as yet untried sniper's rifles with telescopic sights. By regimental command, we were listed as cadets of the regiment's sniper school.

It was hard for me to say goodbye to my mates in reconnaissance, but becoming a sniper was my long-cherished dream. Since child-hood, in fact. And even now I can still recall in minute detail scenes from the pre-war film *Sniper*. It was about the feats of a super-accurate Russian marksman in the First World War. In particular, I vividly remember the scenes from the film dealing with the art of camouflage. By making a replica of a tree-stump or a dead horse and planting it in no man's land a sniper could then climb into it and hit the enemy accurately from there.

Before the war, while still in school and then at the Tambov railway technical school, where I studied for two years, I became keen on shooting. I entered competitions. We had a strong shooting team at Tambov Tech; four of us got into the city team. My friends Anatoly Abonosimov, Mikhail Shtanko, Boris Vavra and I were already practising for the regional competitions. Our team then included the current sergeant-major of the 5th Company, Vlad Dudin, who worked at the Tambov carriage repair shop and was a member of the city council. I had been friends with him since then.

At that time we were not just keen on shooting: long before being called up for urgent service each of us wore on our chests the full range of defence badges – and, what's more, of the second, and highest, stage: PLD (Prepared for Labour and Defence), PSD (Prepared for Sanitation in Defence), PACD (Prepared for Anti-

Aircraft and Chemical Defence), and the 'Voroshilov Arrow'.

'You'll be in charge of the group' the lieutenant told me as he handed over the 'List of personnel in the sniper's school within the 14th, Red Banner, Regiment of the NKVD forces'. Apart from those already named, the list included Valentin Loktyev, deputy political instructor Yuri Smirnov, Sergo Kazarian and others. Vlad Dudin, officially company political instructor and acting sergeant-major, was temporarily appointed as sergeant-major of the sniper school.

Our 'academy' commenced regular classes from morning till night. The cadets strove to acquire as quickly as possible all the tricks of the sniper's art, which Lieutenant Butorin willingly shared with us. On the first night, with an upturned round mess tin pressed between my knees and by the light of a wick made from a shell casing, I wrote a letter. As briefly and discreetly as possible I informed Mum of the change in my life at the front. Taught from childhood not to hide anything from my mother, I was now compelled to write neither the whole story nor the whole truth; I didn't want to upset her again for nothing.

Letter from the front to a mother in Tambov:

> Dear Mum,
>
> There's no need to worry about me. Yesterday, unfortunately, I parted company with my work in reconnaissance and my friends there. A pity; the fellows there were all the right sort. Now I am engaged in study – deep behind the lines – there's not even a whiff of war here! I'm getting used to a new team. But I'm still choosing my friends according to the principle: 'Would I go on a reconnaissance mission with you?'
>
> True, the lads here are also sensible, friendly, cheerful and brave.
>
> Vlad Dudin and I are together as always. You know him. Also here are both the Ivans – Dobrik and Karpov – who I've told you about.

Warm greetings to all our neighbours. Pass on our regards to our school – for all the good things it gave us. It has all come in handy at the front.

> Warm hugs and kisses,
> Your son Yevgeni

# 2.

# I Become a Sniper

Our 'academy' was situated in a convenient gully, not far from Sheremetyev Park. The first half of our day was devoted to practical exercises. We shot with our own weapons, tried to hit the target, and learned the arts of camouflage and choosing one's sniping position. The programme also included physical fitness: running, strength exercises, long jumping and high jumping. Throwing grenades and Sambo wrestling (a Russian martial art) were also part of the training. Once again, just as before the war, only now with even greater effort, we crawled on our elbows and attacked an imaginary enemy. 'A sniper should be hardened both morally and physically,' Lieutenant Butorin told us, as he watched us in action.

Returning from the gully as darkness fell, we would first clean and oil our rifles and dismantle and reassemble them endless times. Taking some oakum and twisting it round a ramrod, we polished the inside of the barrel with an alkaline solution until we had obtained the ideal shine. Lieutenant Butorin introduced us to the component parts of various weapons, both Soviet and captured ones. But special attention was paid to the sniper's rifle and its telescopic sight.

There were also lessons on observation and training one's visual memory. They went like this: a student was called into the dugout by the lieutenant and required to observe a number of objects spread out around and then go out again. In two or three minutes he would return and specify what changes had occurred during his absence. Some of the objects would have been moved or disappeared altogether. All this had to be noted down to the last detail and clearly reported to the lieutenant. Exercises like this developed our powers of observation and sharpened our attention. We ran them on the spot, right on the front line. This training really appealed to all those on the course, although not everyone was successful at the reporting back. As a theatrical artist, it was much easier for me to remember things than it was for others, but, even so, mistakes occurred. However, the essential quality of a sniper is not just to see and observe, but also to draw the right conclusions from what he has seen – this was something we improved at with every passing day. All this came in very useful later. We realised that both our success and our very lives depended on our mastery of these skills. A sniper poorly trained in this respect could become a target for an accurate enemy marksman.

Whatever Lieutenant Butorin explained to us, whatever he taught us, he was always interesting to listen to. He usually illustrated his narration with examples both from his own experience in the Soviet–Finnish War and from that of snipers in the First World War and the Civil War.

The lieutenant knew a lot, and knew how to relate it in a graphic, vivid and accessible way. We heard so much during these sessions that was useful and interesting.

Besides, we had seen a lot ourselves since the Germans attacked us in June 1941. We had gained experience in fighting the enemy – not a lot of it, but the experience was our own. In my case, for instance, I happened to have helped wipe out Finnish snipers – 'cuckoos' or 'suicide squads', as our troops used to call them. Suicide squads in the full sense of the word, having been dropped into our territory and selling their lives for huge sums, they sat chained to tree-trunks and branches in leafy thickets near transport routes behind our lines.

Who chained them there it is difficult to say. Maybe they did it themselves, hoping for heaven knows what. But, well camouflaged and completely invisible, they annihilated our troops and officers one by one in calculated fashion with their accurate fire as they moved from place to place. They took out the drivers of cars and trucks along with their small numbers of passengers. Then they would set fire to the vehicles themselves. On discovering where these 'cuckoos' were from their shots and where their bullets struck, albeit only approximately, we would rake suspected sites with machine-gun fire and destroy them. Occasionally, under cover of our own fire, we would creep right up to the tree where a sniper was ensconced and finish off the pest with hand grenades tossed up into the foliage. We would pull the grenade's pin, but not throw it immediately; rather we waited several seconds. Then it would explode in the air, up where the marksman was positioned; there was no time for it to fall back onto the ground and injure us.

One day, when I was taking part in such operations for the first time, I was surprised that after several grenades thrown by me had detonated in the foliage above, nobody fell out of the tree, as ought to have happened. I decided to climb the tree. Great was my amazement when, taking all the safety measures, I ascended about six metres and ... beheld, almost beside me, a sniper hanging down head first with one foot chained to the tree! And a little higher up, on the same sort of chain, hung his rifle, which he had prudently discarded. I could not reach it, but, feeling that I was now completely safe, I climbed higher. Among the thick foliage he had a well-equipped lair. There I discovered two kit bags. One of them contained not only provisions, mainly tinned food, but carefully-packed bundles of cash. There were enough provisions for at least a couple of weeks. There was chocolate and biscuits, condensed milk, cigarettes and matches, a portable spirit lamp and a flask of fuel for it. In the second bag there was a whole box of cartridges, which had already been opened, and a single grenade. Apart from the cartridges the bag contained empty food tins, boxes and packing paper. There were ordinary and incendiary bullets, as well as explosive ones. Since the beginning of the war I had succeeded in wiping out three such 'cuckoos' on Karelian territory. One of them was a woman.

'A sniper is a super-accurate sharpshooter who takes aim at important targets,' Lieutenant Butorin told us. 'His rifle, with its optical sights, serves as a means of precise fire from close and medium distances at fleeting individual targets, both in the open and camouflaged.' He took his rifle and raised it up high.

> This rifle makes it possible to shoot effectively within a range of between 100 and 1,300 metres. And, without the telescopic sights, from 100 to 800 metres. And, take note, it guarantees good results even in twilight, at first light, and at sunset, as well as in overcast weather. You only have to master it properly. That is your goal.

And we set about mastering it ... After the exercises the trainees would be dropping from fatigue, but later they were very grateful to their strict teacher. In making snipers out of us, the lieutenant did not promise us an easy task. On the contrary, at every convenient moment he warned us of those unexpected and difficult situations in which we might find ourselves.

Having studied the components of our rifles for several days, we also learned how to fire them. At first we shot at paper targets, then at objects of ever-diminishing size. Among them were empty bottles, used food tins and matchboxes. An empty box would be threaded onto to a thin twig or straw stuck into the ground to serve as a marker; the object was to hit the twig or straw while leaving the box undamaged.

Hitting a bottle lying on its side was commended particularly highly. You had to aim so that the bullet would strike the bottom of the bottle and emerge through its neck without smashing the bottle itself. True, not everyone managed to achieve it.

We also shot at moving targets. One of us would walk 500–600 metres away from the firing line and, choosing an uneven patch, drag two or three pots or other objects along the ground by a long rope. They served as stand-ins for the helmets and heads of the Nazi forces. We also practised shooting rapidly; we strove to fire ten to twelve targeted shots a minute. However difficult the instruction was for us, we steadfastly endured it. Finally, the time came for examinations. At the beginning of October, we emerged as a group to take them right on the front line.

At that time the enemy had a patent advantage over us both in manpower and in military technology. Nor did he stint himself in the use of ammunition; to a single rifle shot the fascists would respond with a hurricane of unaimed fire at our trenches. Their dive bombers and other aircraft were constantly overhead, 'working over' the front line.

One day a frenzied Nazi ace who had been unable to get through to Leningrad returned to base with an unused load of ordnance. On the way he decided to rid himself of his bombs and dropped them on our trenches, without, it is true, causing any particular damage. Warned in good time by observers, the troops managed to take cover in shelters.

'Air attack!' shouted the observers again, noticing that the enemy aircraft was turning round. Our trenches emptied, except for our pet cat Mureshka, who had made her home with us and was now calmly crossing the highway in the direction of our neighbouring mortar teams, who, according to their timetable, were due to be serving dinner. Flying along the highway and not noticing anything of interest apart from 'a cat proceeding in single file', the Nazi pilot swooped down on her for his own amusement and sprayed her with a scything burst of machine-gun fire.

Crazed with fear, the cat sat down briefly with her tail beneath her and then dashed along the highway. The pilot did not hesitate to make a third attack and succeeded in killing our Mureshka. The bastard was a deft marksman. However, this sortie proved to be the last one for him too. One of our lads from Tambov, Yuri Semyonov, fired a single shot at the plane from an ordinary rifle and seemingly scored a direct hit on the pilot. Losing control, the aircraft failed to emerge from its last dive. Landing on its nose, it rammed itself deep into the ground and, to everyone's delight, exploded. We rejoiced; our Mureshka was avenged

And so we set off to take the examination. It was a gloomy October morning. The trenches had long been permeated with damp and the cold at night had become more noticeable and palpable. The first significant amount of snow had fallen the previous day, straight onto the dry, frozen ground like a blanket covering the crippled earth of Leningrad. We all realised that our first wartime winter would be very severe.

Dividing our group into pairs, Lieutenant Butorin stationed them to defend the regiment in firing positions that they had earlier chosen. We already knew the evening before who was with whom and where each would stand. Each pair had occupied their site before, put their foxholes in order, and prepared and camouflaged them.

My partner was Ivan Dobrik, a sturdy lad of short stature with a broad, good-natured face, but a perpetual sly expression on it. He was an excellent marksman on the smallest targets and a downright outstanding serviceman. I remember an incident that took place between us during peacetime in Karelia. That evening I was returning to the company from the regimental headquarters.

Standing on guard by the barracks was our Ivan, who knew me like the back of his hand. He thrust his bayonet at me.

'I'm not letting you through. Go see the guard. Why are you late?'

And he would not have let me through either unless, fortunately for me, the officer in charge of our platoon had happened to come out onto the barrack's porch.

And now he and I were lying side by side and observing the enemy defences. Directly in front of us, a kilometre and a half away, was a railway line; we could see a level crossing with a signal box and the barrier raised. This was our principal reference point. Along the highway which crossed the tracks there was active movement of vehicles and German troops in both directions.

Closer to us lay a plain dusted with snow without a single suitable feature to guide oneself by. Somewhere along it were the enemy trenches.

A column of smoke from the stoves of the Nazi dugouts was rising high into the frosty sky and steam was pouring out of the kitchens. Hungry as we were, it seemed to us that the Germans were being fed right around the clock. Through the telescopic sights of our rifles we could see far into the depths of their defences and German soldiers, large as life, both groups and individuals, occasionally wandering here and there, unfortunately beyond the range of our bullets.

We lay like that for a long time without taking a single shot, nestled up against the snow-covered parapet and closely pressed against each other. Lying in the frost for several hours on end without moving was not much fun. And we were not used to it. We were clad in overcoats on top of padded jackets, padded trousers tucked into *kirza* boots (made of a unique Russian form of artificial leather) and caps with earflaps. And still the frost went right through us. We so wanted to get up and warm our frozen feet and hands with some vigorous movement, but we knew this was impossible. We must not reveal ourselves to the enemy who was also watching our defences. We were in a lousy mood. It began to get dark.

As if to spite us, the snow began to fall again in large flakes. Visibility grew noticeably worse.

'What should we do?' asked Ivan quietly in a mixture of Russian and Ukrainian. 'Shall we leave, or what?'

'Better the "or what",' I told him. 'Where do you want to be off to now? To meet a German bullet? It's still light.'

I wanted to add something, but suddenly I noticed some moving targets in my firing sector, about sixty metres from our observation point: three Nazis walking six or eight metres apart. The first one had a woman's scarf tied criss-cross around him and moved unimpeded. The other two were lugging sacks containing some sort of heavy load. For some reason I decided that they must be potatoes, so slow and heavy was their tread.

'Ivan, take a look? I can see some Nazis to the right!' I cried out joyfully, completely forgetting that I was only about eighty metres from the enemy front line and could become a target myself. 'I'll take the last one, then the first one.'

Dobrik had spotted the Nazis too.

'Don't let them get away, Yevgeni!'

Making the usual adjustments to allow for crosswind and the movement of the target, I set my sights on the head of the last of the three Nazis and, holding my breath, smoothly pressed the trigger. The sound of a sniper's bullet is not loud, but its sting is lethal. I barely caught the sound of my shot – my own heart was thumping much more loudly, it seemed to me! I saw the last of the Germans sink down under the weight of the heavy sack. The other two continued on their way without noticing what had happened. Cheered by my success, I decided to shoot the second Nazi. With a well-practised motion, I instantly reloaded the rifle. The second 'conqueror' also fell, as if he had tripped. However, he must have had time to yell something, because the first soldier, who had taken two of three further steps forward, stopped, looked around and went back up to his fallen companion. He stood over him, gesticulating with his hands and saying something to the solder lying immobile. He was possibly ticking him off for his clumsiness or, more likely, suggesting that he get back on his feet, still failing to guess what had actually happened and certainly not expecting what would happen a second later. But I had more than enough time to reload the rifle and take another shot. It made a sharp 'crack' – as if a woodpecker had struck a dry fir tree with its sturdy beak. And felled by my bullet, the third Nazi collapsed dead on top of the second.

'Well done! Three at once! With three shots!' Ivan summed up the results of my marksmanship. 'Now it's my turn. 'And he got himself ready to fire, excited by our initial success.

Without letting my own sector out of my sight, I began to pay more attention to Dobrik's sector. But the Germans did not come that close again. And, as ill-luck would have it, so much snow fell that visibility was completely lost. Even only some fifty metres away from us nothing could be seen. It began to grow dark; the weather had completely packed up.

After lying there for about another half-hour we decided to go back. Disappointed, Ivan trudged behind me along the trench, hanging his head. I tried to cheer him up, predicting a better 'hunting trophy' for the following day. But within ten minutes we were already sitting in our dugout.

Thus, thanks to Lieutenant Butorin, a sniper force was born within our 21st Division. The exterminators of the Nazi plague had begun their sacred war. Late in the evening, when all the snipers had returned from their observation points, the results of the day were analysed. 'The first step is the hardest!' said the lieutenant:

> The result of our exam is twenty-six Nazis wiped out. Not bad! But don't forget, comrades, the field of battle is not a shooting range! A sniper has to have a bold heart and strong nerves. He must always be calm, cool and composed, patient and hardy. Whoever is keener of eye, firmer of hand and stronger in stamina emerges as the victor. The Soviet sniper knows what he's facing and defeats the enemy through his bravery, quick wits and rapid reactions. I'm telling you this for the last time. Tomorrow you'll be operating independently and there'll be nobody to teach you. But now it's time for sleep. May you all sleep through till morning!

After bidding us goodbye, the lieutenant left the dugout. But we tossed and turned for a long time, and could not drop off owing to the impact of what we had experienced. Then one of the lads suggested:

'Listen, tomorrow we should see who can score the most. Like a competition. What d'ye think?'

Within half an hour we were all sound asleep. I was the only one who couldn't sleep, for some reason. Perched on the edge of the bed, I began, by the light of an oil lamp, painstakingly to inscribe a letter on a piece of paper with a well-sharpened indelible pencil.

A letter from the front to a mother in Tambov:

> Dear Mum,
>
> I've successfully concluded my training. Today the officer in charge congratulated to me in front of the assembled troops. Now I have a new job; I have become an observer. Don't worry about me – it's easy work and quite safe: looking through binoculars and reporting what the Nazis are up to. And you get to sit where it's warm, and I'm decently dressed.
>
> There's almost no fighting where we are. When you read in the Soviet Information Service reports 'All quiet on the Leningrad Front. Minor engagements', that's about us.
>
> How are you getting on there? And how are folk in general back there in the real world? We only know one thing: our people will survive! And they will be victorious.
>
> And I haven't told you yet: I've been given a promotion! I am now a senior sergeant – and deputy platoon commander.
>
> Your Yevgeni

From then on we went out every day onto the front line in pairs, or sometimes alone. We would steal up as close as possible to the German lines, settle into our favourite shell hole or other convenient hiding place and, before the sun was fully up, manage to camouflage ourselves, take a good look round and make ourselves at home. The front line was our second home, one in which we spent more time than in our own dugout.

Forewarned by our comrades in the trenches, we would observe snipers and their activities. They had the task of covering a sniper's withdrawal if something went wrong and rendering him first aid if needed, for the mortar bombers were liable at any moment to unleash defensive fire and cut us snipers off.

We were only allowed to sleep at night and we were only woken in the case of extreme necessity. True, there were more than enough such cases . . .

# 3.

# My First Partner

I had further interactions with Ivan Dobrik subsequently. Until he was seriously wounded in the head in September 1942 we fought side by side.

When I went out 'hunting' with Dobrik, I felt more confident. Ivan was a cheerful and courageous lad, a good mate and an excellent shot. You could rely on him absolutely. He hailed from the Poltava region. His home town – the village of Khudoleyevka – was 'under the Germans', he told me in thick Ukrainian and he had not 'heard a word' as to the fate of his parents and numerous brothers and sisters.

It had been difficult for his parents to maintain their simple holding, to support a big family. And after consulting with them, the eldest – Ivan – went off to Astrakhan to find work. He spent time there with fishermen on the Caspian Sea and dragged in nets. But everything he earned he sent back home. He got by with one thing or another. And dreamed of joining the army. Wherever he wrote, whoever he turned to, the army would not take him. 'Too young! Grow up and bit and we'll call you up ourselves!' he was told at the recruiting office.

Indeed, in October 1940, when the date fell due, he was called up into the Red Army.

Although Ivan was sturdily built, had matured over the years over the years spent in Astrakhan, was broader in the shoulders and had grown very muscular, it was not reflected in his stature. He was still rather a short squirt. They sent him to an NKVD regiment. Eternally cheerful and inventive, with a ready tongue, round smiling face and hazel eyes, he was always glad about everything, always happy. Even glad at being sent to a place unknown to him like Karelia. What a lot of interesting things the young country lad saw from his small railway carriage, what a lot of new things he learned along the way! And what a size his homeland must be if it took so long to reach the place where he was due to serve.

After several months in the regiment Dobrik had completely matured – his own mother would not have recognised her eldest in a line of smart, close-shaven lads in uniform. Here Ivan became keen on sport and scored 'excellent' in fire-arms and political training.

As war began, with determined resistance his regiment withdrew from the border into the hinterland. But the Nazis paid dearly for their perfidious invasion. The NKVD troops defended ferociously, each fighting with the power of ten men. But, all the same, the forces were not equal – the regiment was encircled near Vyborg.

Day and night the rattle of rifle and machine-gun fire continued unceasing from both sides. The mortar bombs exploded with a howl. Troops armed with rifles had tanks thrown against them. But this time the Nazis failed to break them. 'NKVD men don't surrender!' – that was the watchword. And the regiment burst out of encirclement and emerged from the battle. Ivan Dobrik was carried out on a stretcher suffering from shell shock.

After treatment in hospital Ivan hurried back to join his mates. With his heart in his mouth he walked through Leningrad to the Kirov works. Ivan walked and saw the way Leningrad residents were helping our troops to strengthen the defences. With picks and crowbars they were striking the rock-hard earth, shovelling out anti-tank ditches and trenches, building dugouts for the soldiers.

'No, people like this will not let the Nazis into their city. So we must hold fast too!' thought Ivan and swore that he would not spare his own life to wreak vengeance on the Nazis for their evil deeds.

In response to an inner calling, Young Communist League member Ivan Dobrik became a sniper. With every passing day his tally of sacred vengeance rose and his mastery of his craft grew and became more refined. The name of Ivan Dobrik, sharpshooter and exterminator of the Nazi plague, began to be mentioned more and more in the pages of military newspapers.

Our trenches ran across some land which, before the war, had belonged to a state farm. The machinery and personnel had been evacuated from it even before the Germans arrived. The only thing left behind was the harvest, which they had not had time to destroy. And so now there was a cabbage field spread out in no man's land in front of our battalion's trenches.

One day a number of women came to the regimental headquarters from Leningrad. They asked to be let through to the front line.

'There's cabbages out there. And our children are going hungry!'

'Do you realise what you are asking? It's in no man's land! It's under observation by the Germans day and night; they'll shoot you straight away,' Rodionov, our regimental commander remonstrated with the women.

'Well, we'll work at night! Then the Nazis won't hit us,' they insisted. 'And your soldiers can help us a bit . . .'

Giving way to pressure from the women, the lieutenant colonel was forced to refer the matter to the divisional commander, Panchenko. He gave the okay but requested that all safety measures be taken and that the women be covered with sniper and machine-gun fire.

And so the following day about twenty of them came, all with huge mattress sacks. The women had a resolute look about them. They knew what they were in for. They had been warned. Right on cue the guard commander let the women into our company's positions and at nightfall helped them to climb over the parapet. And, impressed by the courage of the women of Leningrad, not only we snipers but all the other troops were ready to come to the aid of the cabbage foragers at any moment. Just before dawn the women returned safe and sound, dragging humungous sacks along the ground. We helped them to carry this precious cargo to a safe place.

The following night still more came. We let them through too. Only this time, buoyed up by yesterday's success, they acted less cautiously. Disturbed by the suspicious and noisy activities in no man's land, the Nazis stirred themselves – flares flew overhead. Intense firing began. The Germans had decided that our sappers or scouts were operating in the field and, by the light of the flares, they began to fire at the women. Slowly and smoothly the flares descended to earth. The parachutes attached to them kept them aloft for a long time.

Meanwhile the shooting intensified. We would fire at the enemy gun-ports, guided by flashes of machine-gun fire. Familiar with the construction of German parachutes, the snipers brought down the flares, snuffing them out in flight. Things went particularly well when several flares flew up together: the highest flare effectively illuminated the parachutes of those below hanging against the back sky. The frightened foragers returned empty-handed. We quickly patched up the wounded women and sent them to the rear, while the dead ones remained lying in no man's land. But despite this, the women kept coming for the cabbages.

Once, after one such 'operation,' some of us helped the women to carry their loot. Dobrik stayed behind to keep an eye on the enemy. Dawn was already breaking when, suddenly, Ivan noticed that two women were still working in no man's land. Their tall figures in long skirts and padded jackets showed up well against the lightening sky.

'What's going on? I thought the women had already come back and been escorted to the rear with their cabbages. What's the story with these ones? And they've gone so far away from us,' thought

Ivan, perplexed. 'What are we going to do? Maybe they're not our women?' There was no one for Ivan to consult with. But then he noticed that the women seemed to be having trouble coping with their long skirts. This put him on his guard.

'To hell with it, I'll take a shot at them!' Dobrik decided and shot one of the women in the leg. Lifting up her skirts and screaming blue murder, she ran off, limping heavily on her wounded leg.

'She was limping towards the German side,' Ivan told us later. 'Limp on, you bitch. I'll treat you to cabbages . . .' and Ivan fired in the wake of the disguised Nazi, who crashed onto the ground. The other German had started hobbling away and failed to make it to his trench – and he too was met with the same fate as his 'girlfriend'.

'Bastards! Well, have you eaten enough Russian cabbage now?'

After that the Nazi appetite for our cabbages vanished, while Dobrik wiped out three more Germans the same day.

And so the cabbages remained in the field till deep snow fell and only in winter, when food was really tight, did our troops begin to harvest them. I went out a couple of times myself on these 'operations'. We got some superb dinners out of it.

There seemed to be hardly anything left of the buildings in Klin, which stood opposite our defences in no man's land: all the windows had long been smashed in, the walls were riddled with shell holes, and bomb craters gaped all around. However, the two Ivans were in the habit of walking over to these houses: Ivan Karpov and Ivan Dobrik, the best snipers in our division. They were very fond of this place – from the upper floors there was a magnificent view of the German defences.

Before daybreak they would climb over there, make themselves comfortable, camouflage themselves and observe the enemy. The Germans meanwhile were preparing for yet another assault on our trenches. Not anticipating any danger from these buildings, which were, if anything, closer to their trenches than to ours, the Nazis were gathering strength for another attack. Ensconced in their building, the Ivans could hear the Germans playing harmonicas and bawling songs; their self-satisfied mugs were visible through the telescopic sights of their rifles. An officer with a monocle in one eye and a riding crop in his hand was giving orders. The Nazi mob was only 300 metres away.

Our snipers did not spend a lot of time admiring this 'amateur artistry'. Assigning roles between them, they presented the Nazis with their own 'concert'. First to fall was the officer with the monocle, felled by a bullet from Ivan Karpov. Following him the other ranks began to tumble, precisely posed, as they were, for the gunsights of our exterminators. Having worked out what was happening, the others began scurrying round the gully in a panic, looking for suitable cover. That day Dobrik wiped out eighteen Nazis and Karpov fourteen. But the main thing was that the German operations on this occasion were sabotaged.

The infuriated Nazis were unable to calm down for a whole hour, conducting precise artillery fire . . . but only at the buildings which had long been abandoned by the two Ivans. True, our snipers only just managed to take cover in a cellar.

Upon subsequently analysing the results of our efforts at a meeting organised by the Political Department about the incident involving the Ivans, we came to the conclusion that we should not get too carried away. An initially successful day like that could have ended in tears for them as well. We needed in any event to mark out several extra firing positions and move between them more frequently.

# 4.

# Shoot the Firefighters!

On the night of 3 December 1941, our 5th Company, which was standing by in reserve in the second line of the defences, had been called up in an emergency and urgently transferred to a new sector near Uritsk. This sector, it emerged later, was the hardest one for the regiment to defend. It was situated along a tram line running from Leningrad through Uritsk to Strelna and, weaving here and there, it deviated from the tram line as far as the Gulf of Finland itself.

The dugouts hastily excavated in the tram-line bank were barely covered by puny layers of planks. If a shell exploded nearby, their walls would rock and all sorts of rubbish would pour down from the ceiling: glass, bits of iron, refuse. So you could only sit in a dugout like this with a helmet on. In the ditch to the right of the tramline ran an actual trench 1.5–2 metres deep. It was impossible to dig any deeper; underground water would well up and flood the trench.

The nights at the time were long and dark. The Nazis were afraid of the dark and of night-time visits by our scouts, and therefore they kept the front line constantly under observation. Regularly, every two to three minutes, they would launch flares into the boundless black sky, so that, thanks to the Nazis, no man's land was clearly visible. That suited us; we could economise on our own flares. Audibility was also good at night; it was only 60–80 metres to the German trenches.

If, before the war, a commander had occupied defences on a front slightly greater or less than what was prescribed by regulations, he would have been marked down. Now we were forced to defend a front three times greater than regulations prescribed with half the manpower of peacetime requirements. And yet, however great the extent of our trenches, however thin the ranks defending twenty-six trenches, not once did I come across our friends from regimental reconnaissance. We met when the lads were setting out for the enemy's rear in search of a captured German for interrogation, or when, having fulfilled their mission, they were returning from reconnaissance through our own defence sector.

These meetings were brief; nobody had time, everyone had work to do, and time was of the essence – particularly when it came to having a good chat! But in these cases we managed to exchange brief bits of information: how were things, what was new, what successes had been achieved. My frequent attempts to get permission to prowl around the enemy rear with my reconnaissance friends did not receive the officers' approval. However, from time to time, I was allowed to interact with search groups and support them with sniper fire.

One day the lads set off into the enemy rear to grab a prisoner for interrogation. I received instructions to go with them as far as the enemy front line and, having accompanied them that far, to wait for their return – but, if necessary, to cover their retreat. It was not the hardest assignment, but it was not trivial either: I knew what happened when the enemy discovered scouts. You rarely got back to your own trenches safe and sound, especially if your mission was successful. Only the most experienced, cool-headed and self-possessed scouts managed it.

Having escorted our friends, who had got through the enemy trenches, I lay in ambush in no man's land and awaited their return. The bomb crater I chose turned out to be quite comfortable. On their return the scouts were not going to be able to bypass it and it provided a superb view of the enemy defences. There was no particular need for camouflage; the snowdrifts did it for me better than anyone could.

It was quiet and peaceful all around. I lay patiently in the snow, staring attentively into the darkness. From time to time flares soared up with a hiss from the enemy's side and observers on both sides casually let off bursts of machine-gun fire. Now and again a machine-gun bullet whistled through the nocturnal gloom. It was the usual front-line scene. My ear picked up the slightest stir – every sound coming from enemy territory.

I whiled away the time, mentally calculating my comrades' supposed route down to the minute. But all the deadlines passed and nothing could be heard 'from over there'. On the one hand it seemed that everything was happening 'as rehearsed'; however, a silence like that puts you on your guard. What if they've got lost and I need to wait for them somewhere else? Or maybe they are lying there waiting for a convenient moment to make a quick dash through the enemy front line, and would turn up where we agreed? Or perhaps something's happened?

In the meantime, it had begun to get light, everything around was turning grey, and the silence had become wearisome. The outlines of the Nazi front line were showing up more distinctly. The second line of the Nazi trenches was becoming visible; one could see the smoke from the stoves in their dugouts, while our own scouts were showing no signs of life . . .

I was already becoming seriously concerned when, suddenly, I heard far away some feverish grenade explosions, and then some hurried bursts of machine-gun fire echoing right in the area where, according to my calculations, they ought to be. What's that? Seems they really have got lost! How could that happen? The lads in the group were all experienced, well-seasoned, had an excellent sense of direction in the dark, and were very familiar with the enemy defences. And the officer in command of them was no novice, I reassured myself, but it was all the more incomprehensible what was happening 'over there'.

But 'over there' grenade explosions were resounding more and more frequently, and the chatter of machine guns was intensifying. Pained by my inactivity and seeing no way of helping them, I began firing at the gun-ports of the German pillboxes, from which streams of fire were pouring forth. Several points fell silent for a while. More I could not do, however much I might have wished it, because a big 'extravaganza' began about sixty metres from me – on the other side of the deep, wide ditch or gully dividing our trenches. Along the bottom of this gully flowed a stream, which had not frozen even in the winter. And sixty metres from the gully stood an isolated single-storey and quite respectable looking house, built entirely of wood, with a sloping roof and chimney, which had survived the war by some miracle. I had spent a long time looking at it, particularly since the houses around it had been razed to the ground or torn apart to provide materials for German dugouts. What was in this house I did not know, just as our scouts probably did not know. And now, behind this house, a real battle unfolded.

For some reason smoke suddenly began to pour out of the chimney – thick smoke, which drifted away into the frosty, winter sky. And within a minute or two something around the house itself began to give off smoke, but the shooting beyond it also intensified, becoming disorganised and frequent. Putting all these events together, – the grenade explosions, and the firing, and the smoke from the chimney – I became firmly convinced that this was our lads' work. Now I transferred all my attention exclusively to the house. And there something quite unimaginable was going on.

The grenade explosions had ceased, but the rifle fire had intensified. Still more smoke appeared around the house, actual flames could be seen here and there, and the rifle fire was being discharged in coordinated bursts, seemingly by a hundred marksmen at once.

'The house is on fire!' I thought,' and recognised the organised, coordinated firing smacks of cartridge boxes exploding! But where were the lads themselves? What was happening there now?'

The minutes seemed like hours. At last I saw some human figures moving rapidly from shell hole to shell hole across no man's land. They were all heading in one direction – coming towards me. I cautiously trained my rifle on the first of the figures approaching me.

'Hey, halt! Who's creeping along there?' I decided to speak up and snapped the breech of my rifle shut.

'Friends.'

'Halt, I say. What friends? Password!'

'But it's us, Yevgeni. Didn't you recognise us, or what? Where did you bury yourself?'. I recognised the voice of Senior Sergeant Maximov.

'Get over here, Maximov! Well, what happened to you over there?' I asked him as soon as he slid, breathless, into my crater. 'How did you contrive to bump into Germans?'

'Well, we found out that this house,' and he jerked his thumb back to where clouds of smoke were rising ever more thickly, 'contains a supply of ammunition; a prisoner told us!'

'Well, we decided to blow this temple up. We took quite a detour and that's why we didn't come out where we planned, and got held up a bit. But at least the building's alight! You can imagine how scared the Germans were! With their ammo about to go up any minute! Well, of course, we didn't manage it without a fight.'

'Are the lads all safe and sound? Or . . .'

'All safe and sound for the time being. Hang on, let's count them now,' said the senior sergeant and lay down beside me.

The rest of the scouts were already crawling past us. The first ones were dragging some bound Nazis wrapped up in waterproof capes. Behind them came the rest, quickly crawling on their elbows.

'We've swaddled a couple of them!' said Maximov with a contented air. 'You see, everything in order. All twelve have returned. There's the last officer crawling up now.'

And he began to signal to Junior Lieutenant Vladimirov.

'Loktyev!' Vladimirov stopped the scout bringing up the rear. 'You stay with me! Tell the others to take cover in the trenches. It'll go up any minute now. We're back safe and sound, despite messing things up! Well, shall we view the fruits of our labours?'

He settled down beside me in the crater. After passing on the officer's order, Loktyev lay down beside Vladimirov and from habit quickly got ready to fire.

Valentin Loktyev and I had been at school together in Tambov. True, he was two classes below me, but his sister Lida was in my class and nearly all the boys strove to win her favour. Val himself – a broad-shouldered, sturdy lad – singled me out above the others because I was often at their home; Lida and I shared textbooks, which were in short supply at that time. Val was a sniper now and had wiped out more than a few Nazis.

'Well thank you to the fire,' said Loktyev. 'That's why the Germans retreated so quickly.'

'Oh yes! I'd say you made extra work for me,' said I, seeing three Nazis going down to the unfrozen stream carrying buckets. 'Well, thank you! Otherwise I would have darn near frozen, sitting here with nothing to do!' And I set my sights on one of the soldiers.

'What are they doing – firefighting? Off to fetch water? Shoot the firefighters, Yevgeni,' shouted Maximov.

But I didn't need to be told – one Nazi was already in my sights. I gave them all the chance to collect water, knowing that, with heavy buckets, it would be much harder for them to move and they would walk more slowly.

'Don't get in my way, Val! You've done your job! Let me do mine now,' I told Loktyev, who was also getting ready to open fire on the Germans.

After pausing to think, he agreed, but kept looking through his sights. The firefighters, as Maximov had christened them, had filled their buckets and were already coming up along the slippery path to the crest of the gully. Their black figures were clearly outlined against the snow. My first shot rang out and the Nazi who had reached the crest of the gully first kind of tripped, fell and rolled back down under the feet of the other two. They also rolled back down, the buckets clattering. I did not give them a chance to get up again.

'Well done!' said Maximov and added,' Hang on! There are more coming.'

And indeed three more Nazis were already running towards the gully from behind the house. Each of them had a couple of buckets in his hands. Without looking round, the first of them slid down the slope of the gully, perched on the folds of his overcoat. The second one wanted to follow his example, but, after surveying the scene before him, worked out what was going on and made to turn back. However, the third one, who had been felled by my bullet, bowled him off his feet and the two of them – both the living and the dead – rolled downhill, overtaking their buckets. Meanwhile I occupied myself with the first Nazi. He had also quickly rolled down our Russian hillside. The second one, who had begun screaming blue murder from fright, tried to dash uphill, but failed to manage three steps before it was all over for him.

Up behind the house, which was even more alight, they had decided to apply a different tactic: without waiting for water, they began tossing snow on the fire. I saw a ladder appear on one side that was slightly higher than the roof of the burning house. Two soldiers were already climbing up onto the crest of the roof, towards the chimney. What they wanted to do up there I had no idea, and it wasn't my concern. But following my shots first one, then the other rolled down onto the ground.

The fire was raging all around the house. Explosions could be heard, and muffled echoes in the storeroom itself.

'Well, brothers,' said Junior Lieutenant Vladimirov, 'now it looks as if it's really going to go up. Let's move farther down.'

We all made a quick dive down to the bottom of the crater. And, mouths wide open, we barely had time to huddle together before the air shook with an explosion of deafening power. There was such a thump that the ground bucked beneath us and planks, beams and huge clumps of earth went up in the air, all colliding with one another. All this fell around us with a crash.

We lay there for what seemed about fifteen minutes. But as soon as we felt that the last fragments had plunged deep into the earth and silence descended, we crept out to the surface. Looking round at the landscape, which had substantially changed in the course of these ten minutes, we ran quickly to our trenches. Not a single shot was heard behind us; there was nobody left to shoot. Everything around the ammunition dump, which had exploded into the air, had been swept from the face of the earth. All that remained were a huge dark crater and clumps of fresh, smoking earth.

In the dugout in the evening I marked the stock of my rifle with four normal-sized and six small stars, using white oil paint. They signified that with this rifle I had wiped out forty-six Nazi invaders. It only remained to add some large stars in place of the small ones.

# 5.

# Day-to-Day Life on the Front Line

When sub-units were replaced on the sector where we were located, one or two snipers who had made themselves thoroughly familiar with the enemy defences were left behind as 'over-timers'. Their job was to help the fresh sub-unit to adjust to the new location and come to terms with the environment. But, as a rule, we stayed on as part of this new company or battalion until the next shift arrived. And this was all repeated with the following shift. The troops went on leave, but the snipers continued working without a day off.

The constant bombing raids, the continuous artillery fire, the pursuit of enemy snipers, the possibility that any second you could become a target yourself for an equally experienced German marksman, or perish from a stray bullet or an enemy shell or mortar fragment – all this made for constant tension.

However, none of us whined or complained because we realised that this was what the cause demanded. What is more, we remained on this sector – voluntarily and quite consciously – and continued to strike at the Nazis, sometimes forgetting which sub-unit we were attached to.

At night, when we were off duty, I used to go see my friend and fellow townsman, Vlad Dudin, our company sergeant-major, who had not been relieved on this sector either. I would clamber into his domestic quartermaster's dugout, lie down on ammunition boxes or some sacks and enjoy a nap in the relative quiet, stretching out my weary legs.

Vlad and I had no trouble finding things to talk about. By the light of a home-made oil lamp fuelled by low-grade petrol or fat, we would recall the distant and precious days of peace-time. We remembered our pre-war regiment, the 154th, the border town, and the beauty of the Karelian landscape. And of course we recalled our home town of Tambov, our traumatically short youth, our home, kith and kin. Only we didn't talk about the girls we were fond of – there simply weren't any.

On becoming a sergeant-major Vlad Dudin set about providing his personnel with ammunition, uniforms and provisions. And in his 'personal' time he and I would go out into the front line with a sniper's rifle. His personal tally already ran to about thirty exterminated Nazis.

One time we became so involved in our conversation that dawn had already broken beyond the dugout's closed door. We were reminded of it by our regimental wit and master of sarcasm, Vlad Kozyrev, who had once been a dashing driver. Before the war he had driven the regimental commander, but had incurred a fine and been reduced to the ranks. Bursting into the dugout, Kozyrev shouted at us from the doorway, his eyes sticking out of his head:

'What are you sitting here for, gabbling nonsense, when the Nazis have played such a filthy trick on us?'

'What sort of trick?' asked Dudin in irritation, expecting, as usual from Kozyrev, another prank or practical joke. 'Have you come here just to blather again?'

'I'm quite serious! The Germans have put up a plywood sign with nasty slogans against us. What are we going to do?'

'Let's go, Vlad,' I said to Dudin. 'Take your rifle and we'll see what visual propaganda the Nazis are up to.'

We got to the front line and, indeed, on top of a German dugout stood a plywood sign on narrow poles thrust into the snow. Inscribed on it with charcoal in big letters was:

'Greetings, citizens! Come over to our side!' in ungrammatical Russian.

'Well, Sergeant-Major,' I told Dudin, 'fill your magazine and fire. You take the right-hand side and I'll take the left.'

After six of my shots the screen was leaning to the left; the pole had been broken. Vlad's, right-hand pole was still holding. I had managed to get one shot at it, but Dudin's last bullet did its job – the plywood sign fell face-down on our side.

'That's better! But what were the bastards thinking of? Showing something like that to NKVD troops! And in gratitude to you for your vigilance, Kozyrev, I'll let you into a secret; they want to take you on as a driver again. True, it's just in an ambulance for the time being.'

And in fact Vladimir Kozyrev was soon taken into our medical battalion. We, his friends, were pleased for him; he loved driving and he was excellent at it. And he was a fearless fellow. The number of wounded Vlad had taken to Leningrad! The number of lives he had saved! He drove competently in any weather, dodging artillery fire and bombing attacks. Kozyrev died in Tambov in 1973 while working for the city ambulance service. He had been desperately ill.

'Listen, Vlad,' I said to Dudin,' I've found a good place to sit tomorrow. You know the wrecked tram in no man's land? I've been pottering around there, getting my firing position ready. Today it'll be finished. It's convenient – just a handshake from the Germans, and everything's visible like, as clear as day. I won't cop a single bullet. I've set myself up almost under the tram.'

'Mind you don't slip up,' replied Dudin. 'It's also a good marker for the Germans.'

'I've thought about that, but I'm not planning to sit there more than a couple of days – I'll change my position.'

'Well, good luck,' said Vlad, ladling out the hot soup we had made from the freshly frozen cabbage. I had been sent one day as 'senior forager' with a group of soldiers to no man's land, where the women from Leningrad had been harvesting. We did not have an easy time of it – searching for huge cabbages under deep snow in forty-degree frost and cutting them in the dark and putting them in sacks made from waterproof capes. But we managed to get enough cabbages for the battalion to last us almost a month!

Vlad and I had a real laugh when I recalled my second 'vegetable expedition'. For some reason that night the Nazis were not directing any fire in our direction. But there was a very simple explanation: apart from my group, the Nazis were also working in the pitch darkness – they wanted some cabbages too. When we worked out what was what, it was already too late; both sides had scattered in different directions.

After thanking the host for the cabbage soup I withdrew to my own quarters; before going out I had to check out my 'girlfriend', as we snipers called our reliable 7.62 mm Mosin-Nagant rifle with its telescopic sight. Checking meant cleaning it, oiling it, and, in winter, camouflaging it by wrapping it up in clean bandages, so that it didn't stand out against the snow. Setting myself down on a box in my dugout, I set about this vital task. The soldiers obligingly offered me cartridges from their supplies that were marked in different colours: yellow-tipped ones had a heavyweight bullet; green-tipped ones were tracer; armour-piercing bullets were black-tipped, sometimes with a red body; and a red tip, rarely seen, identified an explosive-incendiary bullet. The Germans and their Finnish allies had yellow bullets which were explosive, the so-called 'Dum Dum' bullets that were prohibited by international law. However, it was just such a bullet fired by a Nazi sniper that exploded in my hand, 'shattering the upper third of the left shoulder', as my medical records later described.

A sniper may go into ambush for a day, but he takes enough bullets for a week – different ones, of all types. Who knows what can happen in the front line over this period! Thoroughly wiping every cartridge individually and placing them in the pockets of my padded jacket and trousers, I also filled up my ammunition belt. As always, I armed myself comprehensively: two pistols – one in the holster, the other in my boot – several hand-grenades, including a couple of anti-tank ones, in my belt, and a Finnish knife. In my shoulder bag was a gas mask. I attached a small sapper's shovel in a cover to my belt – we did not go out on operations without it. I had left a big spade in my firing site, where I was now heading.

I was not weighed down by all this stuff unnecessarily. Like every sniper, I knew that it would be needed at some time or other, especially in the event of a one-on-one with the enemy in no man's land. If I had a supply of provisions, I would not get him. You fight worse on a full stomach; when you have eaten, you relax and feel like going to sleep. And the slightest blunder on the front line may cost you your life. We did not even take water with us when we went out 'hunting'. Weapons, bandages and cartridges – that is what a sniper supplies himself with in the first instance. It is also better to leave your overcoat in the dugout; it is no great effort to make do with a padded jacket – you can move around more easily in it.

It was time to set off, before dawn broke. Everyone in the dugout offered me a warm farewell and wished me a safe return. This had become customary for us; who knows whether you will come back from the 'hunt' safe and sound? But it was not done to voice this aloud – such was the established order of things.

In any case I invariably told the lads where I was going and where I would be sitting. Also informed of this were the company commander, military security and reconnaissance. I was sure that my location and activities would be followed by more than one pair of eyes and this gave one more confidence in the successful outcome of any such operation. You got a feeling that even if your comrades were not at all close physically, they were almost beside you in spirit.

Firstly, military security . . . I sat down, took a breather, and had a chat with the lads, advising them once again to keep an eye on my observation point. They had only just arrived for their shift and would remain here till darkness fell. The rest of my journey

– from military security to the tram – I negotiated cautiously, crawling on my elbows.

And there was the vintage tram – standing like a lonely orphan with no glass in its windows. Its red and yellow sides were pockmarked with bullet holes and smashed through by shell fragments – not a single spot was intact! It was also covered with wood chips. Inside, the wind whistled right through it. It was said that its last run was unsuccessful; all its passengers were captured and shot by the Nazis. First to suffer was the conductor, who was trying to offer resistance. Now this wrecked tram was probably the Germans' number one marker. I had already been here earlier more than once and was familiar with the scene down to the smallest detail.

I settled comfortably into my deep-dug firing position – to the right of the tramline and slightly in front of the tram itself. My observation point was well camouflaged on the side facing the enemy and nothing was likely to be detected from above. Our troops had long been instructed in the art of camouflage, especially we snipers. It is no secret that the casual, slack and careless do not survive at the front.

I did not regard myself as a slacker. Even in childhood – whether at school or home – I taught myself to carry out tasks entrusted to me conscientiously and carefully, even if I didn't like them. My mother worked hard to keep us in clothes and footwear and to provide the opportunity for a normal education. She would come home late from work tired and I always helped her around the house. That is why in the army I found service easier than others who were not accustomed to looking after themselves. And at the front I quite deliberately spared no effort when it came to digging; it was essential for the preservation of your own life. I passed this on to my trainee snipers.

Several more agonising minutes passed, and indecisively, cautiously, as if concerned that his appearance would set machine guns rattling and cause people to die, the sun glanced out. It was now quite light.

I had been studying the enemy defences for a long time. I saw the little mounds so familiar to me in detail – the German dugouts. Now and again somebody would pass by near them, cautiously stooped over. They did not need to worry – it wasn't them that interested me today. I took a look to the rear; according to what our scouts had told me, their headquarters ought to be somewhere there. I tried to locate it. Earlier on, any Nazi headquarters was easy to distinguish by the telephone lines. Now the Germans had become more careful; they had begun to run the wires along the ground and cover them with snow.

I waited for those who were either running or walking quickly. Within a couple of hours, I spotted some and, among them, two or three men who, wherever they went and however long they were absent, always returned to one and the same dugout. I began to examine it – it stood out among the others for its size and height. From the side I could see the door – a big door, like in real houses. On the side facing our trenches there was a window, which was also wide, but low. But the main thing was the sentry walking back and forth by the dugout. 'Looks like that's the headquarters,' I thought to myself, and finally switched all my attention to it.

I estimated out that it was roughly 700 metres away. The human figures were small, but distinctly visible; my telescopic sights magnified them fourfold. But estimating distance by eye is one thing; it needed to be checked! I set my sights at 700 metres and loaded the rifle with a tracer cartridge. Apart from the door I could not find any particularly notable marker. I chose a moment when the machine guns were chattering on the edge of the front line, and, covered by their noise, took a single shot – the bullet left a clear trace to the door. Everything was precisely worked out! Now it only remained to make a slight adjustment to the sight's drum – and await the kill. Today, apparently delivered on order.

Yet my first shot was not at that dugout. Forty metres away from it was another dugout – with no windows or doors on my side. However, I caught sight of three Nazis leaving the white hump of the dugout. One of them was naked to the waist, while the other two were minus overcoats, just in uniforms. Raising up his arms, the half-naked one began to walk around. 'Who is he surrendering to? Bastard, he's come out to do his exercises,' I guessed. The other two began to wash their faces with snow. Waiting for the moment when the semi-naked man finally stopped and began to do some squats, I took my first shot. The Nazi squatted and . . . collapsed onto the snow and lay down, as if he was going to sunbathe, glad to see the bright sun. The other two carried on washing their faces with snow. Then one of them turned, looked at the lying man and apparently said something to the other. He turned round. They both stood there and looked at the man spread out on the snow, then went up and began to lift him up. Then, realising what was up, they started looking round, perplexed, not realising where the bullet had come from. They did not even look at our trenches, apparently thinking that the distance was too far. I did not allow them to ponder too long and skewered both of them.

'Not bad for a start,' I thought and loaded the rifle again. I carefully took three cartridges from my pocket and placed them on a little shelf – to keep count of them. And hardly had I got ready to fire again when I saw a motorbike and sidecar approaching the headquarters dugout.

The motorcyclist dashingly rode up and stopped dead by the door itself. A tall German jumped down from the pillion in no time at all and began to assist a fat Nazi to get out of the sidecar. While he was obligingly fiddling round with this person of seemingly important rank, I focussed on the rider who had learned forward to rest on the handle bars and was not moving. The tall man was still trying to drag the fat man out of his cradle. Eventually he clambered out and began stamping his feet. I fired. Meanwhile the tall man had turned to the motorcyclist, wishing, I thought, to command him to leave, but, seeing that he was apparently asleep over the handle-bars, gave him a nudge – in vain, however.

After my third shot the tall man also fell backwards behind the motorcyclist, waving his arms.

'Right ... suppose we've got another three cartridges!' And I tipped them out of my pocket onto the shelf. 'What are we going to do now?' I said, talking to myself and excited by my success. But events unfolded with lightning speed. I had just managed to reload my rifle and get ready to fire when some more Nazis popped out of the dugout, drawn by the noise of the motorcycle and possibly expecting someone. They were two officers with medals glittering on their chests and peaked caps on their heads. One of them dashed towards the Nazi who had been sitting in the sidecar just a few minutes ago, but was now lying dead on the snow in front of the dugout. The second one shouted something, calling for help from inside the dugout. In no time at all a third officer leapt out and also dashed over to the dead man. They began to lift him up, trying to drag him into the dugout. I first killed the one who was giving orders – I surmised that he was more important than the two who were dragging the fat man. After him, the other two met their deaths.

Enthusiasm is all very well, but the voice of reason was still telling me: 'Enough for today! You can't stay in one place so long – they'll get you!' I stopped firing for a while, but continued observing the Nazis. Whatever happened, there was no way I was going to get out of here before darkness fell.

But not an hour had passed before the Nazis began to stir again. With short dashes, from dugout to dugout, they began to approach the headquarters and the motorbike ... And I couldn't hold back any longer: once again I opened fire on the bandits. First one fell, then another behind him froze to the spot. The others scattered – as if all blown away by the wind! One man tried to start the motorbike – and succeeded. Then two armour-piercing incendiary bullets hit the petrol tank and did their job.

'Eleven in one day! No, brother, you won't post that record without consequences!' And, remembering how I had taught young, budding snipers to be cautious, I not only ceased firing but stopped observing the enemy. I settled down into my deep little foxhole. There's was not much room in there and I was terribly thirsty; I felt the urge for a little sleep – the extra nervous tension had seemingly had an effect. 'So what, I can relax for a little bit.' But I had scarcely closed my eyes before a shell whistled past and exploded somewhere nearby. Leaping up immediately, I looked out of the trench and saw 300 metres away huge clumps of earth settling back from on high.

'Oho, they're chucking the heavy stuff at us! Sounds like long-range artillery – it was barely audible!' I was pleased that the enemy gunners were firing so poorly – they were clearly a long way away, about five kilometres. I was pleased that the shell had exploded not in Leningrad but in an empty field, albeit near our own trenches.

Several minutes later I once again heard the whistle of a flying shell. It grew in volume. The explosion forced me to stoop down lower in my foxhole. This shell fell about 100 metres away from me and closer to the tramlines. Clearly, the gunners were aiming for me! But I never got to hear the next explosion; I only felt the earth shake under my feet, as the third shell landed somewhere nearby.

'Well, come on, come on, you Nazi scum, shell the whole road. Let the Leningraders rejoice at your "accuracy"!' There was only one problem – my tiny nook was crumbling little by little, loose earth was pouring in, my foxhole was growing smaller. It was simply impossible to use a spade now; the Germans would notice. But another exploding shell somewhere behind me and to the left of the tramline forced me to reconsider: 'They're trying to pick off the tram! It's the tram, or rather me, that they're aiming at! This conclusion made me hot under the collar. 'Bastards! They've guessed, the rats! It's too late for me . . .' The next exploding shell tossed up fresh tons of earth. A huge clump, the size of a cauldron lid, covered me in my firing niche, landing heavily on my back. 'It's all over,' the thought raced through my mind. 'I'll never dig my way out: I've got no more strength left, and something's weighing down heavily on my back, and there's earth everywhere – in my ears, in my mouth, up my nose.'

Again some blunt object landed on the ground and something heavy struck me on the head and rolled onto my shoulders . . . Then there was total silence, darkness descended, and I could think no more.

\* \* \*

I came to in our company command post, in a vast concrete pipe laid across the tramline and right under it. I was sitting on a stool with my back leaning against the pipe. Everything on me was unbuttoned, my arms hung loosely like string, my legs were wide apart and there was a buzzing in my head. Some people were walking around me. I sort of recognised them and didn't recognise them – everything was in a fog. They were talking to me – I could see that – but the voices didn't reach my consciousness. 'Maybe I've gone deaf,' I thought.

And so I sat there, obtusely staring at the floor, which had water flowing across it; the floor comprised freshly-cut boards laid at intervals. I could see my officers, a telephonist with a receiver attached to his head and ear, and I could see an oil lamp smoking away on a shell box, which was being used as a table. I was sitting and trembling ever so slightly. There were no conscious thoughts in my head. Then somebody familiar dropped down onto his knees beside me. 'Who does he remind me of? I know him well!' Finally, it dawned on me that it was my friend and fellow-townsman, medical assistant Ivan Vasilyev. Near him on the floor lay an open first-aid bag. For some reason I remember it particularly clearly – it was green with a red cross on the lid. I was trying to gather my thoughts, but nothing came of it, and I closed my eyes and collapsed . . .

After a while I opened my eyes again, but there was nobody around; the scenery was just the same except that the oil lamp was smoking dreadfully and I was choking.

As they told me later, I slept at the command post for eighteen hours uninterrupted, slept as I sat there. Nobody disturbed me.

And only on the following day, when I had come to myself a little, was I told what had happened that day. The German gunners firing at the tram had let off exactly eleven heavy shells at this conspicuous target. The fire came from long-range guns beyond Uritsk and Strelna. Their objective was to wipe out a Russian sniper ensconced in the tram, as they thought. The sixth shell exploded almost beside my observation point, and I was buried alive in my foxhole. And only after the artillery fire was over did our boys with medical orderlies, sent to my aid by battalion commander Morozov and medical assistant Ivan Vasilyev, dig and pull me out of the grave almost lifeless and drag me to the company command post.

'What about my rifle?' Those were the first words that I had uttered – or rather stuttered – for the last two days.

'Enough, my dear fellow! Your rifle is all twisted, bent in three! No specialist will be able to fix it now! Wait for a new one!'

'Well, cheerio,' said battalion commander Morozov. 'Relax. You're going to the regimental first-aid section, and you can lie down there if you don't want to end up in hospital. You're pretty well shell-shocked, so you won't get by without medical treatment.'

That night I was escorted 'deep in the rear' – to the regimental first-aid section, where our own medical assistant, Vera Yarutova, was 'on the warpath'. A courageous woman, she had been involved in engagements from the opening days of the war and saved the lives of many of my comrades.

'Well, sweetie! You're in my hands now! Come on, lie down on this bunk – we'll deal with you right now.' She was doing something to me – massaging my joints, giving injections, setting about restoring my speech.

One pleasant surprise was the appearance of my friend, Vladimir Dudin, in the first-aid section. Sensing that something unfortunate had happened to me and knowing where I was, Vlad had crept in to see me right, and he had himself caught some shrapnel from the eleventh and final shell. I now heard him bargaining with Vera; the conversation went like this:

'Well, your head's going to be all right,' said Vera, as she finished bandaging a veritable turban on Dudin's head. 'Now take your trousers down. Where did that shrapnel get to?'

'Vera, well, Comrade Yarutova! Maybe we can do without that? Why are you making me take my trousers down – in front of a lady?'

'Take them down, you dandy! Where am I going to give you a tetanus injection? And who's going to take out the shrapnel?'

'Comrade medical assistant, dear lieutenant, you might at least turn away, do it by touch.'

We were unable to drop off to sleep for a long time after that, teasing each other and laughing at every piece of trivia. We were enjoying it because we were young, we were together, side by side, relaxing in spite of our injuries. Even now they make us laugh because it is all long behind us. We were only a kilometre from the front line, but we were 'in the rear', lying with our legs stretched out and our boots off, on sweet-smelling hay piled on real bunks, and covered by blankets, which we had not seen since the war began. However, we all had pistols and grenades under our pillows.

Letter from the front to a mother in Tambov:

> Dear Mum!
>
> I am not hiding anything. Honestly, I am alive and well, safe and unharmed.
>
> First I must tell you that Vlad Dudin and I are now on rest and recreation in the rear – it's a kind of gratuity for us. For example, I recently wiped out eleven Nazis in a day – and now I've been rewarded. Yesterday a scout I know dropped by in passing and said that three days ago our troops had captured an important Nazi. At interrogation this man told us: 'One of your snipers killed eleven gallant soldiers of our Reich in two hours. One was a general and the others included two colonels and several officers, who had come from Berlin on the instructions of the High Command.'

So my tally now includes a general as well, with a couple of colonels in my collection.

So you see, I am truthfully reporting my activities at the front. Now I'm waiting for your report on life and work.

Yevgeni

# 6.

# Duel

December was a harsh month. The winter of 1941/42 has remained in everyone's memory; it came early and it was ferocious. There were forty-degree frosts at night and on the plains the snow lay a metre deep. The winter months became a difficult test both for us, the defenders of Leningrad, and for its residents.

However, the brave Soviet soldiers fought unyieldingly under the walls of the city and the courageous folk of Leningrad stood firm. Every one of them regarded himself or herself as a soldier and every soldier considered himself a native of Leningrad. And, whatever the difficulties, we believed that victory would come, that victory would be ours. Soldiers gripped their rifles even more firmly, full of determination to defend Lenin's great city.

Our snipers also began to hammer the Nazis more heavily. The movement to exterminate the German invaders grew and broadened across the entire Leningrad Front and acquired a mass scale. Every division now had snipers whose tally numbered several dozen obliterated Nazis. Whole sections, detachments and even companies appeared bearing the designation 'sniper'.

And the Nazis quickly felt the impact of Soviet marksmen, whose dead eyed firing cost them hundreds of their own officers and men. Now the Germans were not as carefree and cavalier as they had been. They began to act more cautiously, not only on the front line but even deep in the rear; they started digging themselves in more soundly, walked round crouched close to the ground, or else even resorted to crawling.

Unsettled by their heavy losses, the German command was compelled to call in troops urgently from other fronts and direct their super-sharpshooters against Leningrad. So, aces like this, expert masters of their craft, killers with seniority and huge experience, appeared in our area too. We quickly felt the presence of the Nazi snipers; they would fire through the slit of a pillbox and skilfully take out our observers. Now it was also impossible for us to walk freely along our trenches, especially on our awkwardly constructed section of the line. It became more difficult for us snipers to operate. Some lost their lives at the hands of Nazi marksmen. Thus, in January 1942, the life of the illustrious sniper Feodosy Smolyachkov of the 13th Division, was tragically cut short. Feodosy's tally amounted to 125 obliterated Nazis. At a funeral gathering, where they bade farewell to him, the snipers of our division swore that they would mercilessly wipe out the Nazi invaders and avenge the death of their comrade. He was buried not far from where he had fought – in the Chesmenskoe War Veterans' Cemetery. In February 1942, by a decree of the Presidium of the USSR Supreme Soviet, Feodosy Smolyachkov was awarded the title Hero of the Soviet Union. In the Vyborg district of Leningrad a memorial to him has been erected – on the same street that bears his name.

I resolved to test myself against one of the Nazi ace snipers who had appeared in our sector. For three days I sat in the rear of the regiment checking my readiness for the forthcoming tussle. Again and again I would string empty matchboxes on straws and, starting from a range of 100 metres and gradually increasing the distance, snap the straws in two. Feeling at last that I was completely prepared for the duel, I set off for the battalion command post.

'Comrade Major,' I addressed battalion commander Morozov, 'I request permission to seek out the Nazi sniper. I want to get close to him. Do I have your permission? I'm ready for anything; it's either him or me – there's no other way. But I have to go, I have to. Do I have your permission?'

'Well, Yevgeni, if it's a duel, so be it. But remember: we need you to get him. What assistance do you need from us?'

'Give orders to the platoons not to walk along the trenches for two or three days and keep out of the way without good reason. But don't stop firing! Let them shoot at the sky, so long as it's audible. I want the Nazi to be on edge, to look for a target.'

'We'll do that. When are you going?'

'I'm setting off tonight.'

By tracking the path of the Nazi's shots back to their point of origin I came to the conclusion that he was sitting somewhere close to the tram lines, in the broad expanse in front of our 3rd Platoon – to the right of it and closer to the Gulf of Finland, in no man's land. Only from that point was he able to strike across our trench. I presumed that he had not one but possibly two or three reserve positions, but they would have to be on the same side. 'Set himself up nicely, the son of a bitch!' I thought. 'Unable to see the targets, he was firing blindly at the entrances to our dugouts. And hitting soldiers sitting by the entrance, which was covered by a simple tarpaulin. He was firing on the off-chance and hitting the mark.'

And so, clad in a snow-white camouflage smock over my regular clothes, I crawled in that direction one dark and frosty night. By first light I was already lying in no man's land, well camouflaged in the deep snow. I was not concerned about concealment. But would I succeed in spotting the enemy? He would also be camouflaged against the same snow, one imagined, just as well as I was.

The day was spent looking for my opponent. I was out of luck; the Nazi ace did not reveal himself. There was not a single shot from his side – whether because the falling snow got in the way or because he failed to find a target. There was nothing left to do but wait.

And I waited. 'He'll either change his position, or he'll move a little way forward, as I have done,' I reasoned to myself. 'But he is bound to show himself.'

However, it all turned out differently.

The snow had long ceased falling and the frost became more palpable. Lying in the snow in *kirza* boots, even with double foot wrappings, wearing a cap with ear-flaps, but ears exposed to catch sounds, and gloved on only one hand, became unbearable. I had such an urge to stand up to my full height and warm up my chilled feet . . . Then suddenly I noticed, against the pure, eye-stingingly white snow, about forty or fifty metres away from me, a suspicious little spot of something coloured differently from snow had appeared. Imperceptibly brushing off the tears which continually came to my eyes from the frost and the wind, I saw that this slightly greyish spot had begun to move. 'What could it mean?' I wondered. This spot gave me no rest, distracted me from my continuous observation of my opponent's defences. Now and then my eyes would turn in that direction. I kept wanting to see if anything had changed there.

And thus, while pondering and trying to explain the reason for this spot, I lost sight of the most important thing – the thing I had been freezing so long for. But it all turned out to be very simple: beside this little spot on the surface a big one suddenly appeared – in white camouflage. In a trice it crept a couple of metres to the left and disappeared as if swallowed up by the earth. From the unexpected nature of it all and being chilled to the bone, I did not even manage a shot!

To spot a Nazi and let him go! There was nothing I could do now and, until complete darkness fell, there was nothing to be done but agonise over the blunder and reflect on it. My thinking was like this: 'The German of course would not be back till the morning. Either he was frozen or he had decided to change his position. Although, on the other hand, there was no point in doing that today; night was approaching. He was simply frozen. Tomorrow he would be here again because he had not fired a single shot from this position.'

I swung into action. Taking some white twigs, which I had prepared beforehand and taken with me just in case, I marked out my 'dead space' – between where the Nazi had appeared and where he had disappeared. Dividing this distance in two, I determined the centre and the line along which I set up three forks on which my rifle would rest when aimed at the necessary point. And tomorrow all my attention would be on this.

While I was engaged on this, night fell. 'Well, till tomorrow! There's nothing for me to do today,' I decided and, burrowing into the deep snow, I began crawling towards our trenches. Locomotion warmed me up a bit, but not enough for me to get down into the trench on my own. That required the assistance of my friends, who were already waiting for me there.

They literally carried me in their arms to the dugout, as my feet had refused to move: they were frozen and, it appeared, frostbitten; contact with a hard surface caused intolerable pain. And once again my friends came to the rescue; they took my footwear off in the dugout and began to rub my feet with snow and woollen gloves until I felt some pin-pricks. The battalion medical assistant, our very own Ivan Mikhailovich Vasilyev, was consulted.

'Oh dear, no brains,' he said reproachfully. 'That's no way to carry on. You should have smeared your feet with fat before you went out, wrapped them in newspaper, and only then wound on your foot wrappings. But, better still, find some woollen socks.'

'Well, tomorrow, Mikhailovich, I'll do everything scientifically. But today just rub them, make an effort, be a mate!'

It was well and truly night by now. The dugout had warmed up. The firewood burned brightly and the stove hummed away cosily. It became quiet in the deserted dugout – my wartime friends had gone to their posts. Without waiting for the hot soup which had been heated up in a mess-tin and having warmed myself up, I nodded off and slept like a log . . .

On the front line we eagerly awaited the arrival of our cook with dinner or our sergeant-major. They always appeared with two thermos flasks filled with hot food. They came twice every twenty-four hours, but only in darkness – late in the evening and just before morning. For the rest of the time access to us was forbidden.

While one of them set out on his dangerous path with the flasks attached to his back by broad straps, the other would prepare food in the kitchen for the following day. Our cooks feared not for their own lives as they made their way through fire to the front line, but for the flasks, which could be struck along the way by fragments of shells and mortar bombs exploding close by. The path from the kitchen to the company's location was not long, but it was dangerous. And time and again the personnel were left with no food. Sometimes instead of liquid soup we were brought the solid ingredients. And then, if there was anything left in the kitchen, the cook or the sergeant-major would negotiate his tortuous route a second time. It was Sergeant-Major Vladimir Dudin who had the hardest time: the trenches were shallow, while he was tall and unused to ducking low to avoid the bullets. And then he would arrive with the flasks from which the hissing liquid was already spilling out.

Everyone was supposed to get half a mess-tin of thin but hot borsch or soup. Some managed to make two courses out of it: first they would drink the liquid with bread, while leaving the solid matter to provide a second course. Hot tea was poured into the lid of the mess-tin. Sometimes the only thing we had to brew it with was a soaked rusk from the oven.

In the morning I was awakened by the company sentry.

'It's time, Nikolaev, up you get!'

'What, already? What a pleasant dream you've interrupted! I was dreaming of my mother. We were buying rye flat cakes, hot and fragrant . . .'

'Did you get to try one?' asked the sentry.

'You didn't give me the chance,' I answered, closing my eyes again in the hope that the dream would be repeated. But the sentry wouldn't let me – he saw what was going on.

'Enough beddy-bye, Nikolaev. You'll miss your Nazi.'

I leapt to my feet in an instant. It was about four in the morning. On leaving the dugout, which stank of smoke and bitter soot, I was glad to gulp in the pure winter morning air. Stripping to the waist and grabbing a zinc cartridge box of clean snow from the parapet, I had a quick wash. Decidedly woken up after this procedure, I went back to the dugout quite alert. I had to hurry up and get to the spot before the Nazi.

Warming up yesterday's dinner on the stove, I hastily finished the food. As emergency rations I took a 100g rusk of seemingly pre-war provenance. Now I could set out on my journey. First of all, I rewrapped my rifle in clean cheesecloth. Then, removing my boots, I did everything that Vasiliev had told me yesterday: smeared my feet with fat, put on woollen socks that somebody had given me, wrapped them in newspaper, and wound on double foot-wrappings. I put on some different boots which had been specially brought by Dudin – two sizes bigger than my own. 'The main thing is to keep your feet warm,' my mother always said. 'The main thing is to wind your foot wrapping on properly,' the army taught. So, I was no longer worried about 'the main thing'. We had no sheepskin coats or felt boots at that time, and so I dressed as usual with an overcoat on top of my padded jacket and similar trousers. I put the finishing touches to my attire with a white camouflage suit.

Having listened to a heap of useful tips from my friends, I hurriedly said goodbye: 'Must go or the Nazi will get there ahead of me!'

I already had quite a good appreciation of the locality – that comes with being a scout – and therefore I quickly found my 'war path'. From the protected zone to my observation point I literally crawled under the snow. Having reached the spot, I set myself up as comfortably as possible. Slipping a cartridge into the chamber, I laid the rifle on the forks prepared the previous evening. Now I had everything ready for an encounter with my opponent; I just had to wait patiently for first light. Today I would only need to take a single shot. Or not even that. It could turn out that way . . .

Soon it began to grow quite light, and the outlines of the enemy defences became clearly visible. My eyes did not move from the spot where the German sniper was supposed to appear. However,

I had to keep watch in all directions in case something had changed since yesterday. 'If you're in an ambush, the first thing you do is look around. If you notice something different, give it your full attention!' I constantly reminded my students, and I acted like that myself. But today I would need to keep a closer watch not only on my opponent, but also on myself: not to cough inadvertently, not to sneeze, not to sniff. I would even have to breathe more carefully, in a controlled manner, cautiously exhaling into the snow; in a frost like this the breath from your mouth will instantly give you away to the enemy.

That I was facing an experienced foe there could be no doubt, just as it could not be doubted that he was already *in situ*. 'He's outwitted me all the same, the bastard, got there earlier,' I thought, when first light had already dawned. Tears began to form in my eyes from the continuous observation of a single point through telescopic sights. It was the wind blowing straight into my face and the frost. I kept brushing away the tears while trying not to make any obvious movements. The fingers of my right hand, which were constantly ready for action, had frozen. And I began to worry as to whether I would be able to hit the target when necessary. I realised that in duels like this there were no wounded – a sniper, like a sapper, only ever makes a single mistake.

But the time was ticking mercilessly by. Three hours had already passed and, since I had been lying here, there had not been a sound or a movement from that side. 'Where are you, you damned Nazi? Show yourself, just for a moment!' I whispered with my chilled lips. Yesterday I gathered from the excessively puffed-shape under the camouflage that my German was superbly equipped. And the hunch on his back was probably a thermos flask concealed under the white suit. 'A flask indeed. Could do with some hot tea over here!' I thought. 'And I would warm my hands, and the cockles of my heart. No, better a cup of your own, home-boiled, strongly brewed, fragrant, sweet tea, and with a piece of cake as well . . .' I dreamed. And all different sorts of new thoughts about home crept into my head; almost my whole life passed before my eyes.

I remembered Tambov, the days of celebration, and my mother, pottering away before dawn over her simple cakes. How was she managing there now without me? It was difficult, no doubt, but she would not admit it, or complain. I recalled our room on International Street, which was always cold, with hoar frost on the door and ice growing on the window. Brrr! How cold home was in winter! And now I was freezing as well ... The door of the room opened directly onto the street. No porch, no corridor. Mother covered the door with a wadded blanket, but slept herself under a flannelette one, with an overcoat thrown over her feet. I wouldn't mind a wadded blanket here now, to warm myself ... I wonder how she's doing for firewood? Is she buying it at the market again? And the way we walked to school in winter! Each of us had to bring a stick of firewood every day. This was the beginning of the 1930s. But what's it like for kids in Leningrad now? My school ... Where are you, my first school, named in honour of Alexander Pushkin? I remembered the teachers, the kids who were friends. Now all fighting! Where are they now, my 'musketeers' – Igor Petrov, Mishka Laptyev, Kolya Balykov and Vaska Budantsev? There'd been no letter from them. I remembered our classroom – a corner room looking out onto two streets at once, Soviet Street and International Street. I could see myself sitting by the window and spending the whole six lessons observing the bored traffic policeman who had nothing to regulate but a couple of buses and a few trucks and cars passing him at intervals. But what technology! And now? And on the German side? They have more than enough of it. And how did I manage to knock out that whole tank crew back then? That heap of scrap iron was left there by the school near Uritsk, until our fellows grabbed it and dragged it into the divisional yard ...

'*Hände hoch!*' – that was what our 'German lass' at the school, Varvara Afanasyevna Belyaeva, said when she asked us all a question. Our dear form teacher, 'Varvarushka', we called her affectionately ... And what didn't we learn about the German language! What a lot of useful things she taught us! If it wasn't for her interesting lessons, plays in German produced with her assistance on the school stage, and reading outside class, would I know German as well as I do now? How handy it came in on reconnoitring missions! And it wasn't just the German – everything I picked up at school, how useful it turned out to be at the front! I'll go back to Tambov after the war and the first thing I'll do is go back to school and bow at the feet of my teachers – Rosa Izaakovna Zilbergolts in chemistry, Natalia Porfiryevna Ignatyeva in maths and physics, Serafima Petrovna Gavrilovskaya in literature and the headmaster, Vladimir Vsyovolodovich Khorkov, who served in the Soviet–Finnish War. And Professor Yaroshevsky in history. How attentive and observant he taught us to be! He would ask: 'You've been coming to this school for many years, so how many steps are there on our staircase? How many windows are there along the street front?' And we didn't know. But it would be good to come to school with a medal 'For Valour' like Headmaster Khorkov . . . If I could only snuff out that bastard over there. Where is he? Fallen through the earth, has he? Is he going to show up? Or is he counting on me freezing before he does? No, enough tomfoolery! I'll stop thinking of other things. I've heard that's how people freeze, day-dreaming . . . No more pleasant thoughts! I need to get angry now, so I don't freeze! And I'm getting angry, angry at that cautious bandit who has once again not taken a single shot today. Has he sensed something, perhaps? Is he scared? But the winter day is short . . .

I had long been clenching and unclenching the fingers of my right hand; they had frozen and didn't want to bend. And it was so quiet, as if the entire defence force knew about our duel and was keenly listening to find out who would fire first. And the German must be looking for me. I had not taken a shot for over a week and he had noticed that and was being careful. I didn't have time to complete my thought, when something seemed to prod me in the very heart: 'Watch out!'

And with good reason: the head of a Nazi had appeared from out of a trench above the snowy covering. All at once I felt hot.

Now, just like yesterday, he would drag his large body out of the trench onto the surface, swiftly cover the three metres distance, and be off! No, you must be joking, you rat, it won't work this time! And I firmly grasped the rifle in my hands.

The Nazi's face, firmly held in the sights of my rifle, was distinctly visible through the eyepiece. His eyes looked furtively at our trenches, from which he could naturally expect all sorts of unpleasant things. He did not even glance in my direction. 'That means he can't see me and he doesn't imagine there could be anyone here apart from him. That's good!' I thought.

I could have pulled the trigger and fired, but I didn't feel like doing that; for then the Nazi would fall into his trench and that did not suit my plans. I had to bring him down and show everyone that he was lying fallen on our land. And I was almost certain that any second now he would leap out. He was all ready for it and he had no other course. He was bound to repeat his manoeuvre from yesterday. Only now I knew about it and was expecting it.

Unsettled by the silence around and hurried along by the intensifying frost and gathering darkness, with one short jump the Nazi landed up on the surface of the ground. Stooping low, he managed to take his first and last step. The shot long awaited on our sector resounded. Like the crack of a whip echoing in the frosty air, it brought the Nazi down onto the snow. His rifle, now a danger no longer to our troops, slipped out of his hands and fell at the feet of its dead owner.

'Well, that's that, it seems . . .' I thought with relief. I felt like standing up, straightening up and yelling out to the whole front line: 'Take a look, fellows, at the bastard of a beast I've laid low!' But I could not stand up and I was still less capable of yelling; dropping my head onto my hands, which were still gripping the cold rifle, it seems I fell into oblivion. The hours and hours of lengthy nervous tension had taken their toll. My whole body was locked by some sort of inexplicable weariness; for some reason I just wanted to eat and sleep, and for a long time, to sleep without waking with a sense of duty fulfilled.

I don't know how long I lay there, only that at some point I woke up and opened my eyes.

'I have to do something. How much time have I lost?' I asked myself. 'The Germans could grab their sniper any minute, come looking for him. No, I must do something.'

I looked in the direction where the Nazi was lying. 'I was wrong to imagine I could miss. That could not have happened!' I thought with relief and began to concentrate on myself. Removing the woollen glove from my left hand, I began carefully rubbing my right hand with it. Then I began to rub it with snow and again with the glove. I rubbed and rubbed, more and more intensely pressing on the fingers until I felt a pleasant prickling sensation in them. And then another rub with the snow. As soon as the circulation was restored in my fingers and my feet, which I kept moving, they began to respond. I crawled over to the dead man without waiting for darkness to fall. I was not afraid of being spotted by the enemy; my camouflage and the deep snow would protect me from the naked eye.

I crawled the forty metres which separated us in the space of a few minutes, sweating profusely as I did so. Overcoming the nausea rising in my throat (it's not every day you have to touch a Nazi you have killed!), I pulled myself over towards his head and immediately saw on his temple the entry wound from my bullet. On his cheek there was congealed blood which had frozen in the icy weather.

For a minute I paused to think: what to do next? Drag the German whole into our trenches as material proof of my deed or sort him out here bit by bit? 'No, there was no way I could drag that frozen bastard the whole way. And who needs him? I'll take what I need and that will be that!'

With my Finnish knife I slit open his camouflage suit and immediately saw that he really did have a thermos flask attached to his back. A flat vessel, of unusual shape, painted white. I removed it and turned its owner onto his back. Under his new white sheepskin I discovered a field bag and a clipboard. And a heap of decorations on his uniform. I cut off these decorations with the knife and gathered all the documents, letters and photographs from his pockets. In the field bag I found some Dutch chocolate, Turkish cigarettes, an Austrian lighter, German biscuits, an Italian safety razor and other stuff. The watch on his wrist was Swedish. 'What an internationalist! Been everywhere and plundered everywhere!' I decided to take his rifle and binoculars. Now everything was ready and I could set off. It was not worth tempting fate any further. But at that moment the muffled buzz of a telephone came from somewhere. 'Just look what comfort he lived in, the bandit!' I thought and I decided to acquaint myself with the Nazi's lair and at the same time, just for the hell of it, reply to the call.

First of all, I noted that, as I thought, they had not dug a passage from the trench to the firing site – a distance of three metres. So they were responsible for his doom. His firing site was no more than a spacious pillbox on top of a foxhole. The observation slit was curtained with a double layer of cheese-cloth and everything outside was covered with snow. Just imagine trying to locate it from 200 metres away! Inside, apart from the telephone and the stool on an actual wooden floor, everything was like our facilities. Only a bit more spacious, and the entrance was covered with a warm blanket.

The telephone kept buzzing. It was persistently demanding that the marksman respond. I picked up the receiver.

'*Was wollen Sie*? (What do you want?),' I asked politely.

'*Wo ist du*? (Where are you?)'

'Oh, go on with you . . .'

'*Was, was*? (What, what?)' resounded through the receiver.

'That's right, not us but you!' I answered with a pun on the Russian word '*vas*', which means 'you', and put the receiver down. 'Time to run,' I decided and, cutting the wire, took the phone with me.

Tired and sweating, but happy, I collapsed into the arms of my friends. Those arms carefully let me down into the bottom of the trench. Having watched the duel for several hours, my friends now hugged me and congratulated me on the victory.

'Quiet, you rascals, the party will begin right now. Let's run for it!'

My warning of a 'party' was timely and the lads quickly understood. Experienced folk! We all made our merry way along the passage to the headquarters dugout with the trophies in hand.

Informed of my return by telephone, the company chiefs gathered at the command post; alongside the company commander, Lieutenant Butorin, sat Battalion Commander Morozov, Company Political Instructor Popov, Battalion Medical Attaché Ivan Vasilyev, and a smiling Major Ulyanov – from the divisional political department. I was not a bit surprised at the presence of the last of these; Major Ulyanov often visited us on the front line and now I was glad to see him. The major was liked and respected for his simple approach, for his courage and for his humanity. Tall and thin, he walked around the front line with a stick; he had recently been wounded in the leg.

'Comrade Major! Your order has been carried out; the Nazi sniper has been eliminated!' I joyfully reported to Battalion Commander Morozov.

'Well done. So, you did it in the end?' he said, embracing me. 'Thank you on behalf of the service. You can have two days' leave. You've earned it!'

'I serve the Soviet Union!' I replied loudly and cheerfully. 'I've been dealing to those vermin and will continue to do so day and night and I will definitely be teaching our whole company how to go about it!'

I remained undisturbed for exactly two days. Carefully tucked up on something soft at the command post and covered with a fur coat, I spent this time sleeping. Neither a squall of artillery fire on our trenches that night nor the call of Sergeant-Major Dudin, 'Time to get up, Nikolaev. Dinner's ready!' were able to wake me. For the first time, it seems, I was making up for all the sleep I had lost while we had been on this sector.

# 7.

# An Arduous Battle

In December 1941 I was appointed commander of a rifle platoon in our own 5th Company, in place of the lieutenant who had been killed in the last battle. But I would not part with my sniper's rifle. Every now and then I went out onto the front line. Taking one of the soldiers along with me, I would teach him the sniper's art, train my successors if you like. My tally was increasing slowly but surely. Also growing in direct proportion to it was the number of stars on the stock of my rifle, which I carefully traced with oil paint. There were now seven medium-sized and six small stars, adding up to the seventy-six Nazis in my tally. It was a brand-new rifle issued in place of the one that had been smashed under the tram.

December 13th 1941 began as usual, with checks on the sentries, compilation of the duty roster, issuing of orders and carrying out commands from on high. Then suddenly a telephone operator from the company command post, Junior Sergeant Filatov, burst into the dugout.

'The company commander wants to see you, Yevgeni. Urgently! He said to drop everything, without delay.'

The company commander, Lieutenant Butorin, had given orders as follows: 'Go quickly to the regimental general staff. Get there any way you can, but you'll have to slip through before nightfall. Go straight to Regimental Commissar Agashin. You need to be there by three o'clock.'

Weaving my way along the trenches, and stooped over as well, was not a pleasant experience. Apart from that I was hungry; there had been no issue of dry rations . . .

Try as I might, I still could not make it by 1500 hours. I was not reprimanded for this; they knew what it was like getting out of our sector in daylight.

'Now dash over to the divisional staff and you'll meet our people there. Report to Matveyev, head of the political section.'

It was also quite a distance to the divisional staff. Of course there were no vehicles along the route – the highway was under German observation and was even shelled at night. And yet, within a couple of hours or so, I was standing outside divisional HQ, trying to tidy myself up. I had had occasion to visit it before – for a snipers' conference, a gathering of Nazi-killers. And quite recently we had been accepted here as candidate Party members: Dobrik, Karpov, myself and some fellows from other regiments.

There were ten to twelve people gathered in a small space outside Divisional Commander Colonel Panchenko's office. Apart from Captain Treshchev, deputy head of the political department for the Young Communist League, there were two scouts present, some sappers and some tank crew. While waiting for the divisional commander, we speculated as to why such a varied collection of people had been assembled here. Finally, we were invited into the office.

'Take a seat, comrades,' said the divisional commander. 'Our conversation will be brief: you are being summoned by the army commander, General Nikolaev. Why, I don't know myself. Each of you has received a personal invitation. At 1800 hours you must all be with him. There's not much time left. You will travel in an ambulance; it's already waiting. You will be escorted by Captain Treshchev.'

At precisely the appointed time we were invited into the commander's office. Its occupant was standing by the writing desk, slightly bent over and leaning on it with both hands. In accordance with the established army custom, we lined up in single file. After greeting the commander, each of us in turn introduced ourselves, taking one step forward as we did so.

Indicating for us to sit down, General Nikolaev picked up a pencil and, moving a large pad closer to him, said: 'I'm going to ask you all for your ideas on the situation in the Uritsk sector: what are the German forces there, how are they acting, what's new in their defences and weapons? I'll ask you in turn.'

And it instantly became clear what was required of us. We were all from regiments stationed near Uritsk. Our regiment, being right at the end of the line, occupied the ground between the Gulf of Finland and the Pulkovo Heights to the left. Uritsk lay directly in front of us . . .

As briefly, specifically and in as much detail as were able, each of us reported what we knew and what we would like to see. And we all wanted to see one thing without exception – the Nazis driven out of Leningrad as quickly as possible. The state of our present position stuck in everyone's craw – inconvenient, exposed, swampy, and easy for the Germans to observe and shell. Everyone wanted some real action. That was why we reported everything as it was. And, indeed, who other than us scouts, sappers and snipers had a complete knowledge of the enemy defences, which we observed every day and studied in detail? Who other than us had got to know the entire front line, no man's land and the enemy rear by crawling all over it on our bellies?

After listening attentively to each of us and remaining silent for a little while, the commander posed one question for all of us at once.

'The picture is clear, Now I want to ask you one thing: can Uritsk be taken by storm? Without stalling the advance unexpectedly? What's your opinion?'

'Absolutely,' we replied, almost in chorus, 'only, of course, with the proper preparations and collaboration between the different kinds of units!'

The commander got up. We leapt to our feet as well. The general thanked us for the chat and shook everyone's hand in farewell. Except that he missed me out and went back to his desk. He picked something up from there, turned to face us and said:

'Well, comrades thank you for your service! And you, Comrade Nikolaev, on behalf of the Military Council of the Forty-Second Army, I am rewarding you for your active extermination of the Nazi vermin with a watch engraved with your name,' and, holding out a small box, he shook my hand.

'I serve the Soviet Union.' I replied with some agitation.

When he had given the order to 'stand easy' and we had left the office, the lads asked me to show them the gift. It was a large pocket watch from the Kirov Factory. Engraved on the inside of the lid was: 'To Comrade Nikolaev, Y. A., from the Army's Military Council for military distinction in fighting German Fascism.'

The lads looked at the watch, read the inscription, and congratulated me, though none of us could have imagined what fate had in store for me and this watch in the not too distant future.

We returned by the same route, by way of the divisional HQ, but now in reverse order of seniority. At the divisional staff and in the regiment they showed interest in the content of our conversation with the general, examined my watch, and read the inscription on the lid, but nobody asked: 'Aren't you hungry, lads?' Of course we were not counting on an invitation 'to dine with us' – it wasn't the time. But they could have let us off a bit earlier . . .

I covered the route from the regimental general staff to the battalion command post at maximum speed – such was my desire to get back quickly and have something to eat. But it was not an easy path and involved travelling some distance along winding, snow-covered frontier roads.

'It looks like something's under way,' I thought, hurriedly making my way through the company's dispositions via trenches which had changed noticeably in my absence; there were empty zinc cartridge boxes lying around by the dugouts, oiled wrapping paper from grenades rustled underfoot and soldiers were keenly checking their personal weapons.

The company commander, Lieutenant Butorin, whom I notified of my return, hastily gave the order: 'Hurry to your platoon. Orders have come down – we attack in one hour.'

'As long as I've got time for a bite before the battle,' was all I could think about, not doubting at all that my platoon was definitely battle-ready and thirsting to get into the forthcoming operation. And indeed the section commanders were distributing the remaining grenades, checking every soldier's weapons and equipment once again.

The Red Army troops were gathering up their humble belongings and putting them away in kit bags which they slung on their backs for convenience, writing quick letters to kith and kin – brief, hurried, and, possibly, the last letters of their lives. I also managed to pen a bit of a note back home.

Letter from the front to a mother in Tambov:

> Dear Mum,
>
> It's still all quiet and peaceful here – as always. Today we're about to move to another area. That should be a lot better than here. So I don't have time to write now, but, as soon as we move, I'll write straight away. I can also tell you that I've been presented with an award – an engraved watch from the army commander.
>
> Regards to all, keep well and don't pine if there are long gaps between letters. With the move and a new postal service anything can happen.
>
> Love and kisses once again.
> Yevgeni

The unit commanders were already reporting on the readiness of their personnel for battle. They had been ordered to check that troops did not hang round the trenches for no reason, nor excessively attract enemy attention, but rather relaxed in the dugouts.

There were still five minutes to go before the agreed signal.

'If you could just give me something to fill the gap,' I said to my orderly. 'I've hardly eaten for two days.'

'Damn it all!' said the orderly. 'How did we manage it so badly? You realise, commander, it's our fault; we thought you wouldn't be coming back! We waited and waited, and then we ate everything up. Please excuse us, commander! But there some letters for you – three of them, and all from Tambov.'

He reached into his gas-mask bag and pulled out three envelopes bearing that handwriting that was so familiar and dear to me. 'From my mother,' I realised, overjoyed. 'I'll read them later, when I'm on my own!' And I thrust the envelopes into the pocket of my padded trousers. I also put my watch there, in a special little pocket to the right, after I had taken a final glance at it. Five minutes to go until the signal.

Then it came, that long-awaited minute which charges you up for the whole battle: three rockets hissed up into the frosty sky, illuminating the snowy plain beyond the parapet, first green and then red. I jumped over the parapet, leapt to my feet and stood up straight, looking round at my platoon. Our trenches were empty.

'Forward! For the motherland! Hurrah!' I cried, and a loud 'Hurrah' of many voices resounded in peals along our front line. The battalion was moving into the attack

Our company burst into the first Nazi trenches without a pause and almost without losses. And, without being aware of anything, without seeing anything but the backs of the fleeing enemy, without paying attention to the chatter of machine guns and grenades exploding underfoot, the company took possession of the second line of trenches and then, hard on the terrified Nazis' heels, of the third line as well. Wielding bayonet and rifle butt, it finished the scum off, using hand grenades to smoke the Nazis out of their strongly built dugouts.

'Well done, fellows! Hit the Nazis harder! Don't look back!' cried Lieutenant Butorin, who had turned up in our platoon. 'The only way is forward!'

And, feeling that the main objective was achieved – the enemy trenches were in our hands – the troops tore after the commander. Leaping over the parapet of the last trench, we ended up in a flat field covered by a metre of snow. Surprised at the unexpected silence and unable to see ahead of us either the enemy or our own neighbouring forces to left or right, the platoon pressed on towards the snow-covered heights, galvanised by the company commander. The others began to finish off the Nazis who had retreated into their dugouts. There were dead Nazis lying in awkward poses all over the place. There were a lot of them.

Restoring order in the occupied trenches, the rest of the company followed its commander and also ended up in the snowy field, ready to strike at the enemy rear. But at this point the Germans, who had come to their senses, launched defensive fire. They directed mortars and artillery at their former trenches and dugouts.

'Forward! Everyone, forward! Don't stick around. Get out of the firing range!' shouted Lieutenant Butorin, leading the men farther and farther away. But there was no quick way of getting to the little hills that offered salvation; the snow was too deep. Just as if they were bound by ropes, our legs could barely move in the snowy mass. On top of that there turned out to be ice under the snow! Two or three shells dropped on this snowy plain and threw up fountains of water mixed with ice and fragments from the shells themselves.

With a single grenade and pistol I ran alongside the company commander. Ten metres away from us Filatov, the big strapping Siberian lad from the next platoon, was running with a DP machine gun at the ready, gamely ploughing his way through the snow. Behind us there were ten to fifteen troops advancing.

'Hey, we're looking a bit low on numbers!' I thought, glancing at our rows of soldiers, which were thinning with every passing minute. 'What's the company commander going to take on now? What are we going to do next?'

And, indeed, what could we do? We had fulfilled our objective, even done a little bit more than that – ended up on the third line of trenches. We did not have the manpower for anything more. Nor the necessary liaison with the battalion. But the most frightening thing was that it was now dawn and our troops were perfectly visible to the Nazis against the snow. The three of us had almost run as far as the hill that promised safety, when, unexpectedly for all of us, the broad black slit of a gun-port opened up at the top of this hill and a frightening burst of machine-gun fire issued forth from it. The Germans sprayed the entire frozen lake with streams of fire.

'So, it's not just a hill, it's a well-camouflaged firing point! A camouflaged pillbox! That's why our scouts failed to spot it; it never functioned, being situated in the depths of their defences!' In a matter of seconds only three of us remained alive on the snowy patch: the company commander, machine gunner Filatov and me; we had ended up in the dead zone, right under the gun-port, which was continuing to belch out lethal fire.

I tried to get up to the gun-port from the side, but I could not manage even two steps before I rolled back down. The pillbox was covered in ice. Getting past it from the rear meant exposing yourself to being shot at point-blank range.

'What can we think up? How do we get out of here?' I wondered and looked round at the snow-covered field. The bright winter sun blinded the eyes. And we were stuck in this dead zone that was marked out by a shadow falling from the hill-cum-pillbox. Suddenly, in the area where the shadow came to an end on the snow, three shadowy figures sprang up. They all grew larger and larger and then finally stopped and burst out laughing, then began jabbering something and gesticulating. As I understood them, they were looking down from on high and rejoicing at the sight of our soldiers dying in the field.

I could not stand it any longer. Without a word I grabbed the machine gun from Filatov's arms, moved back a little to the side, and focused on the three jolly officers on the crest of the hill. They were tall, standing in a row, and roaring with laughter. My fingers pressed the trigger and a short burst silenced the three wags for ever.

'Well, lads, we'd better get back to base. One by one. Filatov, you cover us with the machine gun!' Lieutenant Butorin decided. 'Let's do it in short rushes, zigzagging and without bunching up. Well, off we go!'

He went first, weaving across the snow and stooping low, towards the safety of the trench. It was only a distance of sixty metres, but it seemed endless. Filatov set off running and ducked for cover, and I dashed after him. Bullets crackled overhead and underfoot – the Nazis in the pillbox had noticed us. With a few short bursts of fire Filatov kept them quiet for a while, and this was when the lieutenant and I made a run for it.

'No, we're not going to make it! And what about Filatov?' I thought, and then I saw that Filatov was also running. Streams of fire issued forth from the gun-port and the lieutenant fell. Was he wounded or dead? I sent Filatov over to Butorin.

'Quick, get to the lieutenant! If he's dead, bring him back. Don't leave him there. And give me the machine gun. I'll cover you. Well, go for it!'

I grabbed the machine gun off him and opened fire on the gun-port. Their machine gun fell silent. I kept my eye on Filatov, who crawled towards the lieutenant, loaded him onto his back and crawled back to the trench, clearing the snow with his hands. Firing back at the enemy, I didn't allow the gunner in the pillbox to raise his head. The pillbox fell silent – for ever, it seemed. But my joy was premature; the Nazis launched a heavy mortar bombardment on the lake. The target was us three.

Mortar bombs were exploding right beside us, squelching up ahead and to the side – and all around us. Suddenly one of them exploded right on the lieutenant's back. Butorin and Filatov had perished. 'It's all over. Now it's my turn!' I realised that it was impossible to get out of this hell alive. Only by a miracle, if such things happen. And I kept running, covering my head with the round magazine on the machine gun. I ran weaving back and forth, trying to get out of the fire zone – to the left and to the right. But the Germans were using their fire to cut me off from the trench, which was only twenty metres away. But just try getting there! 'Any minute now, any minute now they'll wound me. But where?' I was still debating with myself. I was afraid of being wounded and agonising in pain, maybe becoming an invalid. 'No, my head is covered by the magazine disc. In the leg? But then I won't get to the trench at all! I don't want a wound in the leg. Better in the arm. But which arm? If it's the right arm, how will I support my hand. Better in the left arm!' And I carried on persistently dodging from side to side away from the blasts pursuing me. The mortar bombs exploded, raising fountains of snow and ice, scattering fragments of metal and debris. I was running through the middle of these explosions and managed to notice that Filatov was moving. 'Filatov's alive! Crawl over, dear chap! Maybe the lieutenant is still alive,' I was thinking and then suddenly I felt a dreadful blow in the left arm. 'What bastard has hit me? Who could have done it?' I was trying to put two and two together. Then I realised that there was nobody around me and that there could not have been. 'So it's me who's wounded! In the arm! The left one,' it dawned upon me. I glanced at my arm as I ran. The sleeve of my padded jacket was ripped to shreds around the shoulder, and my palm felt warm and damp. An explosive bullet, it would appear. Who could be firing when the Germans themselves are not to be seen? A sniper?'

It was painful. The arm was dangling. But I realised that the sniper had to be taken out; he would not let Filatov crawl away. I lay down in the snow and got ready to fire the machine gun. Where and at whom I could still not see. I thought that they were again firing from the gun-port. There was nowhere else! I aimed, fired, but did not hear a shot. I pressed again and again, with the same result. Out of ammunition! Of course. How many cartridges could there possibly be in one magazine?'

Overcoming the pain in my arm, I crawled towards the trench. I could not abandon the machine gun, even with an empty magazine. It was a weapon! So with the machine gun on my arm I collapsed into the trench. Somebody grabbed it from me and someone tied a narrow strap around my arm, stopping the blood.

'Orderlies! Are there any medical orderlies here?' I shouted at the soldiers. You need to help the machine gunner to drag back the company commander. Somebody help Filatov!'

Finally, I came to myself to a small extent and began to make some sense of what I observed around me.

'How many are left alive? Which of the officers?' I asked the soldiers. They told me that none of the officers were visible and there were very few troops.

'Listen! You all need to prepare your weapons, and grenades. The Nazis may attack. We mustn't let them into the trenches! Find some medical orderlies! We must help the wounded and send them off to the rear. Find some rope or telephone cable in the dugouts. We need to toss it over to Filatov. He won't be able to crawl here on his own.'

I felt they were listening to my orders and that my 'musts' were being accepted as obligatory. Someone was already bringing a reel of telephone wire. Filatov was lying ten metres from the trench, covered by the lieutenant's body.

'Filatov! Are you alive? Can you crawl?'

'I'm wounded. Help me! I won't make it on my own!'

'Right away. Catch, Filatov! Hold on to the end of it and twist it round you. We'll pull you along! Don't throw off the lieutenant!' I cried and for some reason fell down myself onto the parapet . . .

The pain had come suddenly. It had pierced my body with burning needles and then retreated, and was fading somewhere. A while later I heard a conversation, familiar voices, but I could not understand who was talking to whom:

'Where shall we send him? He's unconscious! Or leave him with the medical battalion?'

'No, off to the Monastery with him, No. 1170, urgently! Hurry up, Vlad! But carry him carefully. Don't shake him, or he might not survive!'

'Who are they talking about? What's happened to them? And where am I? What's happened to me?' I was trying to understand but nothing made sense. I got the impression that I had been picked up and carried somewhere. Then I heard a familiar voice and some very familiar words:

'Well, brother, look after yourself! Get well and come back to the regiment! We'll be waiting for you!'

'Brother . . .' Who talks like that? It's Vlad Kozyrev's voice! It's him all right. The door of his ambulance slammed and he was off to fetch more wounded. And I lost consciousness again.

# 8.

# An Unusual Operation

The huge evacuation hospital No. 1170 in the Monastery of Saint Alexander Nevsky was full to overflowing. I lay on a stretcher by the wall in a long corridor. Maybe it was because the stretcher was resting directly on the floor that the ceiling with its arched vault seemed so high up. There were draughts all around, or so it seemed to me, and my teeth were chattering.

Striding along the corridor and gesticulating vigorously was a tall, slim man in a snow-white smock with the sleeves rolled up to the elbows. Tripping along beside him and explaining something as she went was a short, grey-haired woman. They frequently stopped by the stretchers and glanced at some papers thrust under the heads of the wounded or else chatted briefly with them before going on their way. They also approached me. Pulling back the blanket covering me, the tall doctor began touching my stomach for some reason. I was shivering from the cold and I felt very unwell.

'Get him straight onto the operating table!' he snapped at the grey-haired woman.

Even now, when I had no awareness of my own body but just a dull pain in it and felt a certain indifference to everything happening around, I experienced a jolt of fear on hearing words that were new to me: 'operating theatre', 'onto the operating table', 'ward', 'injections', and so on, not having yet experienced their true significance. In the meantime, a sort of tall, white, cold metal table on rubber wheels, with handles just like a stretcher had been wheeled up to my stretcher and stationed alongside.

'Move him carefully; it's a stomach problem!' someone ordered.

I remember that I tried to roll over from my stretcher, which had been raised by the orderlies to the level of the table, but I felt such a hellish pain on lifting myself that I immediately lost consciousness. . .

I was floating in some kind of fog. Then it dispersed, and suddenly a woman in white appeared beside me. Except that she was not floating, but sitting beside me.

'You've come to, son? Thank God for that!'

'Who are you? And where am I?'

'Don't get up. Lie quietly. You're in the Shock Ward after a serious operation. I'm going to call the doctor over to you now.' And she got up off the chair.

'Wait a minute? What does "shock" mean? Why am I here?' I was already scared by this unfamiliar and, it seemed to me, frightening word.

'Don't get upset! It's all behind you now. You should be glad!'

I was tormented by nausea. I could not feel any pain but I could not move – as if tied to the bed. 'Maybe I really am tied down.' I wanted to move, but . . . I was falling somewhere.

I came to as the result of a loud conversation, from a familiar male voice:

'Well, where is my hero? I was told he'd woken up.'

Standing near me were several people in white gowns. One of them was the tall man I had seen back then in the corridor.

'Have I lost a lot of blood or something? And will my arm be usable?' I asked.

'He doesn't seem to understand what's happened' said the surgeon and laughed cheerfully. 'We are together today with this dear man,' and he indicated somebody standing behind him, 'and you've been operated on. And some operation! Completely unique. A shell or mortar fragment had driven your watch into your stomach. It was left strewn all over. And we've been gathering up the components with a master watch-maker. He told us which were missing and I searched for them and extracted them. All the screws and springs that were in the watch, we've got them all out! So you can thank him; he's a good master of his craft. Well, now you must relax. You need to sleep a bit more.' And he moved on to the next bed, telling the sister along the way what more needed to be done for me.

So, now collating everything that had happened to me over the last twenty-four hours and what was gradually but episodically drifting back into my memory, it all became clear: I had been wounded twice – in the arm and in the stomach. I was tired from the lengthy conversation with the doctor, although I had not spoken but merely listened. And, closing my eyes, I sank into oblivion, into good, tranquil sleep.

Within a few days I felt significantly better and I had already got to know all the doctors, sisters and nurses. And not only in our surgical department, but with others who had simply walked in to our 'shock' ward. They often stopped by my bed, talked to me, and praised the golden hands of the surgeon.

The details of the operation which this cheery man and superb specialist had carried out were known to the entire hospital. Except for me. Now they took pleasure in telling me about it. It happened like this. 'Straight onto the operating table!' I had heard. But when they had sorted out what was what, the surgeon said: 'I can't manage without a watchmaker! Find one quickly!' Where they found one, and so quickly, nobody knows, but they came up with a good specialist. With his assistance all the tiny components of the watch had been extracted from my stomach along with rags and wadding from my trousers – all the glass, all the screws, all the springs and cogs. True, along with them it was necessary to remove part of the bowel, but such are the costs of production . . .

What saved me, according to the surgeon himself, was the fact that my stomach was empty, devoid of contents. That made his work easy during the operation. For my recovery I am indebted to the hospital's conscientious sisters and nurses, who looked after me. To all of them, who put me back on my feet and gave me a second life, I will be grateful to the end of my days. And I got my engraved watch back again later, and not just one watch! I received exactly the same kind of watch, with an engraved dedication from the Political Administration of the Leningrad Front in January 1942. It was presented to me by Mamlyakat Nakhtangova, who had visited our 14th Regiment with a delegation in August 1942 – the same Mamlyakat who had learned how to pick cotton expertly while still a little girl, and had received the Order of Lenin and a gold wristwatch from Stalin's own hands. And my stomach healed. True, it is still sore to this day, but that is probably only natural. As the doctors say, some 'repair work' continues to remind you of its presence.

When I arrived in Leningrad in January 1964, on the twentieth anniversary of its liberation from the blockade, I counted on meeting the people who had saved my life. However, my quest was unsuccessful; fate had scattered those who survived the war to the far corners of our vast homeland. Where are they now? Homage to them, the medical staff of the Leningrad Front – the surgeons, who worked through air raids and shelling, the medical personnel, living and dead, who perished from wounds and hunger while saving the lives of hundreds of thousands of people during those unforgettable 900 days of the siege. From us front-line troops, our mothers, and the wives and children of our soldiers – a big thank you.

# 9.

# We Were Young

Eight days had passed since I had arrived in the Shock Ward. Slowly but surely my ills were abating and my strength beginning to return. The efforts of the medical personnel were assisted by my youthful constitution. Now I finally believed that I would live.

Along with my health a positive disposition also returned. There was time for reflection, for making sense of everything I had endured over the months of war. After life in the trenches it was a pleasure to lie on a real bed, on a soft mattress, and under a sheet that might not have been snow-white but was absolutely sterile.

I greeted every morning gladly. I enjoyed the prospect of being allowed to get up soon, of walking around, breathing fresh air, returning to my own regiment and to my wartime friends, and being able to hold a sniper's rifle once again. The only thing lacking for complete happiness were letters from my mother and the beloved girl I had failed to meet along the way in my twenty years of life. I had no intention of writing home that I was wounded, and seriously so, and currently lying in hospital – no need for my nice, kind mother to worry about that.

With a capacity of only four beds, our ward was never empty. In the space of twenty-four hours one or even two of the beds might be remade a couple of times, as the occupants changed . . .

It depended on the nature of the wound, the character of the wounded, and principally on his personal discipline in the ward. If he found within himself the strength and stamina to fulfil the doctor's orders for six days after the operation, he survived. If not, he was transferred 'downstairs', as we put it, to the basement. That happened, for instance, to one man with a serious stomach wound who, unable to endure the thirst tormenting him, contrived to swallow several mouthfuls of water while washing . . .

One morning, following the doctor's rounds and the usual hospital procedures, I had managed to nod off again when I was woken by an unfamiliar but very pleasant female voice. I opened my eyes and my sleep vanished like magic; standing by the door of the ward was a twenty-year-old girl of short stature. Far from being just nice looking, she seemed to me to be amazingly beautiful. Under her white medical gown one could easily tell she had an attractive figure. The small black shoes on her feet gleamed with lacquer. Personally, I was accustomed to seeing our girls in boots, and these neat little shoes particularly astounded me.

But not only me; the whole ward was now gazing enchanted at the newcomer.

'Which of you is Zhigaryov?' the girl asked, looking closely at each of us. She asked this question twice, incidentally. 'What, is there no Zhigaryov?'

'Here I am!' said the middle-aged soldier called Vasily Zhigaryov, finally coming to himself.

'So you're Zhigaryov?' she asked again, approaching his bed. 'Then take your documents and sign right here.'

And after handing something over to Uncle Vasily, she said goodbye to everyone and left.

'Who is that beauty from who just came into the ward, eh?' I asked with a stunned expression.

'Things are looking a bit brighter, eh? Haven't you noticed?' said my neighbour in the next bed, in reaffirmation of my sentiments.

'If I could just make her acquaintance!' I thought, and decided to make inquiries.

'Sandra, who was that who came just now for Zhigaryov?' I asked our ward sister, Sandra Nevzorova, as disinterestedly as possible.

'That's our Tina, the civilian sister from registry. Why? Has she taken your fancy?'

'And what does she do in this registry?'

'Looks after all your things, and documents. If anybody needs anything, you can apply to her.'

'In that case she's the person I need. How do I find her?'

'Well, it's too late today, but tomorrow I'll ask her to call on you in the morning. What did you want?'

'Well, it's just that ... ' I stopped short, 'I want to ask her to bring my wallet to check if everything's all there.'

'All right, tomorrow I'll bring her to you, Nikolaev.'

Of course, for the rest of the day the conversation was only about her. We remembered peacetime, our families, friends, those close to us. We indulged in boasting where we could – some with photos, some with letters from their beloved. I had nothing like that to show.

The next day I woke up earlier than usual, two hours before it was time to get up, and began to wait. However, she turned up only after the doctor's rounds.

'Who wanted to see me?'

'I did! Come a bit closer, please,' I said as calmly and earnestly as I could, although my mouth was melting in a smile. 'I can't see or hear you very well.'

She came up to my bed. 'What questions have you got for me, comrade patient?'

'Sit down here, please, and I'll explain it all to you now, Tina!' Summoning up courage, I took pleasure in pronouncing aloud that name which I liked so much. 'I want to ask you to find my wallet.'

'All right, I'll go and look for your wallet. What's your surname?'

'My name is Nikolaev! Yevgeni Adrianovich Nikolaev! Date of birth 1920, sniper of the 14th Regiment, senior sergeant.'

Within half an hour she was handing me my own wallet:

'Is this yours? Take what you need, and I'll put the rest back.'

'You know, Tina, I'm sorry, of course, but this is not my wallet! Mine's not like this; it's a bit bigger, also black, but a little newer than this one . . . '

'That's impossible!' she said in exasperation. 'I couldn't have mixed them up! That's never happened . . . All right I'll go and have another look.'

'Wait a minute, Tina! I wanted to ask you something else: you couldn't help me write a letter to my mother, could you?'

'All right! I'll finish my shift and call back. So, your wallet's bigger than this, you say?'

A few minutes later she returned with another wallet, which was, of course, not mine either.

'You know, Tina. That one's not mine at all! Seems I didn't take a proper look at the other one.'

'All right,' she answered patiently. 'I'll bring the other one back again, and you can take a look at it. But that'll be a bit later.'

By evening we were already real friends. And I found out a lot about Tina. She lived with her mother right there, at the hospital. Her mother worked as a senior departmental sister. Her father was a distinguished seaman. She had a fiancé, and his name was Fedya. He was away fighting somewhere, only not on our front. There had not been any letters from him for a long time, and she did not know what had happened to him. But no, she did not take offence at my tomfoolery with the wallet, when I told her frankly that I just wanted to get to know her.

'Tina, you don't play chess, do you? If you like, I'll teach you and we could have a game.'

'All right, only tomorrow. I'll be completely free of duties. I'll get a chess set and bring it along. Well, are we going to write this letter?' she reminded me. 'I've found you a real envelope and some good paper.'

She crouched by the bedside table and got ready to write:

Letter from the front to a mother in Tambov:

Dear Mum!

Don't be surprised that I am not writing myself. It's deliberate!

I'm back on a training course again. I'm living in Leningrad. I sleep in barracks, on a real bed, just like in peacetime!

How long I'll be here, I don't know yet. Possibly a month. I'll find out in the next few days and write.

I've got to know a nice girl here. We've become friends. She's called Tina, and her full name is Melitina Nikolaevna. I would like to show her our town of Tambov after the war. Maybe she'll like it? She's already promised.

'What's this you're making up, Yevgeni? I'm not writing any more! There's not a word of truth in the letter. How can you do that? And what is it you're saying I've already promised you?'

'I can and I have to write like that right now, Tina! You've no idea what my mother's like. She'll walk all the way to Leningrad if she finds out that I'm wounded. Why upset her? Let her have a peaceful life; it's not easy for her as it is. So, shall we carry on?'

'Go on, then . . .'

Well, Mum, that's enough for today. We'll write more often now: both on my own and together with Tina. Write to her address. She works in the hospital next door.

The whole hospital loved Tina. And it was impossible not to love her. I loved her too . . . But, knowing about her fiancé, I did not confess my love. I jokingly called her my little sister, would not let anyone upset her, and did not upset her myself.

Later, when I had recovered and returned to the regiment, Tina and I often corresponded. And whenever I happened to be in Leningrad on army business, I found time to call in at the Monastery of Saint Alexander Nevsky and visit Tina and her mother. They would serve up a hot drink and I would bring some treats. But first I had to tell them how many Nazis I had wiped out over that period. For them that was the most precious gift.

Tina and I parted unexpectedly; her Fedya turned up, and she went off urgently to see him in unoccupied territory. He was wounded and lying in hospital somewhere. She managed to leave me a short note. I did not blame Tina for dashing off. I had no right to. However, I really missed her for a long time, that nice girl with the blue eyes.

When you are at the front and doing something difficult, when your life is in constant danger, you really long for someone who is dear to you and loved by you, someone for whom you would be ready to go to any lengths; someone for whom you'd do only good things. To this day the image of my first love is sacredly preserved in my memory. She helped me to continue living during the most difficult period of the siege.

# 10.

# An Unexpected Meeting

On New Year's Eve 1942, I was transferred to a hospital on Borodin Street, a building which, before the war, had housed a school.

I was still weak, the stitches had not yet closed up the gap in my stomach following the operation, and the wound in my arm was not healing well. But by the middle of January I could already sit up, and then I began to get up and gingerly move around.

The small ward of the hospital's surgical department, where I had been put, was bright and cosy. There were three others there with me. One of them was Major Pyotr Antonovich Glukhikh, investigating magistrate of the Leningrad Military District. The second was the principal surgeon of this hospital. He was slowly dying from emaciation and physical exhaustion. The third bed in the ward was occupied by a fair-complexioned lad of sixteen, a civilian. They had recently amputated his left leg, which had been injured in an artillery bombardment on the city. Restless like all boys of that age, our Sergei cheerfully hopped around the ward from bed to bed on one leg without crutches and even managed to get out into the corridor in this way, against doctors' orders. Sometimes he forgot that his other leg was not there and fell down, losing consciousness. The stitches, which had not had time to heal properly would burst open and blood would flow. We were amazed that there was a drop of his own blood left in our Sergei's body. His face was white, like a new pre-war sheet.

Eventually there were only two of us left in the ward – Pyotr Antonovich and I. Our neighbours had been taken away. They did not come back to the ward of course ... Pyotr Antonovich was walking wounded, and gradually I began to go out into the corridor myself. I found it difficult with nothing to do – I was not used to it and therefore tried to find myself any work that was going. I enjoyed for instance helping the sister on duty, whose desk stood almost by the door of our ward, to compile graphs, reports and other hospital documents.

I became particularly friendly with one senior sister from our surgical department, the universally-respected Alexandra Ivanovna Kropivnitskaya, who was a member of the city council. She devoted all her time and energy to the hospital. I would often sit with her and her daughter Lena, who was a first-year student at the Leningrad Medical Institute and almost the same age as me, by the duty sister's desk in the corridor and talk about all sorts of things. Lena and I quickly found a common language. Energetic and lively, with a sharp tongue, she was the favourite of the wounded men. She would read the paper to them, write letters home that they dictated or simply chat with them.

Lena once told me that she had found another man from Tambov in the hospital. It turned out to be our sergeant-major, my friend Vladimir Dudin. He was on the third floor (I was on the first), all entangled in a complex contraption of wires, bandages and a heap of weights – lying crucified, buried up to his neck in plaster. It took a lot of courage to lie like that for so many months. But Vladimir had an abundance of it.

He appeared to be feeling fine – smiled with his white teeth and made jokes as always.

'Well, Vlad, you haven't forgotten how to laugh. We'll live another day, eh?'

'You can't break us Tambov folk! We'll fight again!' replied Dudin.

I perched myself on the edge of Vladimir's bed and in no time at all we were absorbed in the old game of: 'Do you remember how . . . ?'

One day I asked Lena to take me outside, into the frost – I felt like breathing some fresh air. She got me some clothes and led me out by the back entrance. We had scarcely stepped onto the snow before, to my great shame, I almost fell over – I was clinging onto her shoulder before I had managed to take even two or three steps.

'Never mind, never mind. It will pass! That's the fresh air, from not being used to it,' said Lena.

My trance-like state indeed did soon pass and we slowly headed across the whole yard along a path she had already trodden, out the gate. We stood there for a little while. But I saw a lot in that short time and only now, it seemed, did I realise what a real tragedy the siege was. Several loaded trucks drove past us. They were carrying the dead. Young and old, men and women, children, frozen, dead in their apartments from hunger and cold, killed on the streets by fragments of Nazi bombs and shells, pulled out from under the rubble of collapsed buildings before they could get home from work . . .

'Let's go, Lena. I've had enough,' I said, my voice becoming hoarse.

I had an agonising desire to get back to my regiment as soon as possible, in order to take my rifle up again and wreak vengeance, vengeance, vengeance on the Nazis for all the sufferings of Leningrad's residents.

One day the ward sister of our surgical department led me into her office:

'Get dressed, patient!' and she pointed to a new uniform lying on a chair.

Failing to understand anything, but accustomed to accepting orders, I put on the diagonally woven tunic, dark blue riding breeches and fine leather boots.

'Just like being inspected by the bride's family!' I thought. And I was not far off the mark.

'Are you ready, bridegroom?' asked the sister, viewing me critically from all angles, and added: 'And now let's be off.'

'Where to, sister?' I asked in a timid, unpleasantly ingratiating, voice in the hope of finally clarifying what all this meant.

'We're going to see the head of the hospital.'

'Why him? Is it to be discharged?'

'The more you know, the more you age!' she snapped back.

The sister opened a door bearing a plate reading: 'Hospital Director' and, letting me through first, reported:

'Comrade Director, patient Nikolaev delivered as per your order. Do I have permission to go?' and, having received permission, she went out again.

I stood there, stealthily looking around. In the office were the hospital director and two strangers – tall men in white smocks, but slung over their shoulders.

'Come over here, Nikolaev, and take a seat!' I heard the hospital director's voice. 'Tell your comrades here how you are feeling.'

'Very well, Comrade Director. I'm healthy, I can almost move freely and I urge you to send me back without delay to my regiment in the 21st Division.'

'Hey, you're out of order there! You can't walk properly yet, and you're still weak, and the stitches haven't knitted. Comrade Colonel,' the hospital director turned to one of the two officers who were not familiar to me, 'today he's not fit to travel, but in a couple of weeks he'll be fine.'

'Well, glad to make your acquaintance, Comrade Senior Sergeant. Get well soon! We'll call on you again,' said the mysterious colonel. 'But in the meantime you are free. Relax, Senior Sergeant!'

Ten days went by. And once again the senior sister brought me the uniform, only now she gave me an overcoat as well, a hat with ear-flaps and some fur gloves. I was beginning to feel nervous. I fussed around for a long time, sewing a fresh collar onto the tunic and fitting the red triangles of a senior sergeant onto the collar tabs of the overcoat as well as the infantry emblem – a white enamel target with a pair of crossed rifles on it. Then I polished every button till it shone. And now everything was ready. We went down to the exit.

A black GAZ-M1 saloon car from the Gorky automobile works was standing there. The back door opened and somebody called out, 'Get in, please. We've been waiting for a long time.'

I struggled to climb in and sat down. Beside me sat the two colonels already familiar to me. We greeted one another like old acquaintances. 'Let's go,' one of them ordered the driver. 'Step on it, but don't shake the car too much.'

Darting off, the car sped confidently along the snow-bound, frozen streets of Leningrad. As is customary for a scout, I looked out the side windows along the way and tried to remember some distinctive landmarks. 'Please may I ask, where are we going'

'What a curious fellow! But don't you worry. You'll soon find out everything.'

The car stopped. Everything around was under a camouflage net. 'When have I been here? When did I see this before? Why do I know, but don't remember?' These thoughts ran feverishly through my head. 'Two pavilions, so simple and expressive in form, of excellent proportions ... It's the front entrance to the Smolny Palace!'

'It's the Smolny, comrades!' I blurted out with relief. 'I remember this building from pictures and films. It's the Smolny.'

'What, you recognised it? Well done! Have you had occasion to visit it before?'

Both colonels smiled, seeing me embarrassed and pleased at the same time.

'No, Sir. Never before. But here, in front of the façade, there ought to be a statue of Lenin. Where is it?'

'Covered with sandbags, protected from artillery fire. As soon as we get the Germans out of Leningrad, we'll bring him out again! Let's go, comrades.'

Climbing up the broad staircase, we went past the duty officer, who saluted us, and two Red Army men who were standing with machine guns by the entrance to the building.

'The major's on his feet! There's something up ... But it's not surprising now that the general staff of the Leningrad Front is here.'

The colonel said something to the duty major and presented a document. The other nodded in assent.

'I'll go and report,' said one of 'my' colonels and went up the stairs somewhere.

'We'll go too, Senior Sergeant. We'll wait for a bit in the reception room. They'll soon call us in,' said the other colonel.

We waited about seven minutes, no more.

'Well, let's go, Nikolaev,' said the colonel. I got up, smoothed down the creases in my tunic behind the belt, patted my hair down somehow, and stepped through the wide open door.

We found ourselves in a spacious office. I took a look around. Between two windows against the far wall stood a large desk covered with green cloth. On it lay a massive malachite writing set. Along the walls were glass shelves filled with books and above them portraits of Marx, Engels and Lenin. By the table were two leather armchairs and, between them, a small polished table.

The occupant of the office stood leaning over the table and carried on writing something on a pad. He looked at us, silently beckoned us to come closer and at the same time, without discarding his pen, which continued to write, he clearly indicated that we should wait a second and keep quiet. Having finished his writing, he straightened up, placed his pen on the black inkstand and said, 'Do excuse me. I'm finished now. So, you made it.'

'Yes, sir! Your order has been carried out, Andrey Alexandrovich. Have we your permission to leave?'

'Yes, thank you, Comrade Colonel. You are excused.' Then, turning to me, he said calmly: 'Well, greetings, Comrade Nikolaev. Have a seat here and make yourself comfortable.' And he extended his hand to me.

I shook it and suddenly, quite inappropriately, I stood to attention and blurted out:

'Greetings! Thank you, Comrade ...' and I stopped short, not knowing what to say further. I did not have the right to call him Andrey Alexandrovich like the colonel and I did not know his surname. He was not wearing a distinctive military uniform, which would have saved me by giving away his rank. The host himself came to my rescue, seeing what kind of situation I was in:

'Zhdanov – Andrey Alexandrovich if you like,' he introduced himself. 'Now, let's get to know each other, Comrade Nikolaev,' and again he extended his hand towards me. 'Nice to meet you!' he repeated once again. He sat me down in a plush armchair and sat opposite.

For a minute we just sat there, closely studying each other in silence. He was apparently giving me the chance to come to myself and not hurrying me with what he had to say.

Before me sat a thick-set man of short stature, aged about forty-five, who had seemingly lost quite a bit of weight. He was clad in a khaki trench coat with an Order of Lenin on the breast. He had a straight nose, a small black moustache and hair of the same colour. There were bags under his eyes from extreme exhaustion and lack of sleep. His eyes were large, intelligent, serious and at the same time kindly and appealing.

Andrey Alexandrovich smiled, and I clearly recalled his face, which I had frequently seen in portraits, and felt timid: 'How did I fail to recognise him at once? That's him, the very same Comrade Zhdanov, member of the Politburo of the Communist Party's Central Committee, Secretary of the Central Committee and First Secretary of the Leningrad Party regional and urban committees, and a member of the front-line council!'

Zhdanov smiled without a word as he beheld my embarrassment.

'Well, do you feel a bit more at home now, Comrade Nikolaev?' he said at last. 'I'm sure you feel much more at ease on the front line! Never mind. Don't feel embarrassed. I've heard a lot about you and what you've done and now an opportunity has come up for us to talk a little in real earnest, as it were. Well, tell me about yourself: how's your health, how's your treatment going, how's the war going, how are the Germans behaving on the front line? You can see how many questions I've got for you. Now try to answer them.'

'Very well, Andrey Alexandrovich. My health is excellent, my treatment is going well in the hospital, so I'll soon go back to my own regiment and fight the Nazis again like before . . .'

'Give me a little more detail about your experience, how you began wiping out Nazis. And about yourself as well. I understand that before the war you worked in the theatre? As an artist?'

'How does he know that?' I wondered in surprise. And, pausing a moment to think, I began to tell him.

I told him about myself and about my mates. I tried to be brief – just to cover the most important and interesting facts. Andrey Alexandrovich listened closely without interrupting me, except that, when he wanted something clarified, he would ask questions and steer the course of the conversation. He was interested in everything, it seemed: what the food was like, how we were clothed, what our officers were like, and much more besides. He was very easy to talk to.

'Well, did you find things difficult at any time? Were you afraid?'

'A bit of everything, Andrey Alexandrovich. After all, a sniper is still a human being with all his weaknesses. You feel a bit frightened at times, when you are going head to head against a Nazi. But it passes quickly. Especially when you see his face up close and you think, that's not a human being before you but a bandit and a beast. You get angry straight away and forget about everything else. The main thing is to overcome fear if it appears. Then everything becomes simpler and easier.'

'And from what range do you usually fire? How close do you get to the enemy?'

'That depends on the extent to which you can outwit him. And, of course, the location makes a difference. My favourite range is 60–100 metres from their trenches. The closer you are to the Germans, the safer it is, in my view: you have a good view of them and there is a guarantee that you'll not be hit by a German shell.'

'You wouldn't like to write all this down, would you, Comrade Nikolaev? So that your experience would be available to our entire front? And not just our front. Let others learn from you. Whatever you can manage. In your own words and focussing on the most important. Don't worry about the rest – our political personnel will assist you.'

'I'll try, Andrey Alexandrovich, although, apart from essays at school and articles for wall newspapers, I haven't had occasion to write.'

Comrade Zhdanov looked at his watch and said: 'Well, we've had a good talk.'

He pressed a button and in came a girl wearing a neat lace cap, like a waitress in a cafeteria. She gave Comrade Zhdanov an inquiring look.

'Nina, some hot tea for us, please!'

I felt embarrassed: 'Don't bother, Andrey Alexandrovich. I had a solid meal at the hospital just a little while ago.'

'No, no . . . Today you're my guest. And don't make up stories. I know how "solidly" you would have eaten!'

Without a word, Nina went out and came back with a tray. On it stood two glasses of weak, but hot, tea. There were two tiny jam dishes, each of which contained a couple of pieces of sawn-off lump sugar, and, on small plates, two slices of black, 'blockade' bread. These slices were so thin that, when I picked up one of them, it disintegrated in my hands and would have fallen back, had I not grabbed it in time.

I drank the hot tea with pleasure and thanked Comrade Zhdanov for his hospitality.

'No, thank you for your fine service to the homeland and for your exhaustive account,' said Andrey Alexandrovich. 'On 22 February we will be holding a rally of front-line snipers. I hope you will take part, Comrade Nikolaev. But in the meantime get better, get yourself completely well again. And don't forget about my proposal to share your experience,' he said, getting up. 'We need it so much, right up to here!' And he expressively drew the edge of his palm across his throat. 'So, I wish you success! Come when the manuscript's ready, call on me directly. Ask for whatever help you need. Don't be bashful. Just telephone. Here are our numbers just in case.' And he held out a sheet from a writing pad, on which two telephone numbers were written in large, legible script. 'And I'll take care of the rest. Well, all the best!' Again he pressed the invisible button on the desk.

This time my escort came in.

'Comrade Colonel, please take our sniper friend back to hospital in a car and do as I instructed. Set up all the proper conditions for Comrade Nikolaev; he has an important and urgent task ahead of him. You will continue to mentor him. I have given Nikolaev your telephone number.'

'Yes, sir, Andrey Alexandrovich! It will be done!' The colonel clicked his heels and stood at attention. 'Permission to leave?'

'Please do. Well, once again I wish you success! We've had a good talk, relaxed, and now we'll set to work' And Comrade Zhdanov again shook my hand in farewell.

'Well, let's have it! Where have you been!' My ward-mates pounced on me with their questions.

'At the Smolny. I had tea with Andrey Alexandrovich Zhdanov.'

'Really? What did you talk about? Don't keep us in suspense. Tell us.'

They listened to me attentively, without interrupting, and only when I had finished my story did the hail of questions come: how did Comrade Zhdanov look, how was he dressed, how did he talk to me, and so on. They were interested in everything!

I willingly answered all their questions; I wanted to relive it all again myself, so that I would remember this meeting for the whole of my life.

The same day they brought me a pile of exercise books with pages of squared paper and ten Tatika brand pencils. I was advised that, depending on my requirements, a typist from the hospital accounts section would be at my disposal.

I took to the work with enthusiasm. Not only did I have to outline everything intelligibly, it had to be done within the time limit. No question, it was not the easiest assignment for me.

During all the time I had free from medical procedures, including sometimes at night, I would sit in the ward or at the duty sister's desk in the corridor, writing intensively. I wrote about what I knew, what I had lived through and endured. I put down everything, it seemed, as I knew best. I cited examples from the life and work of our snipers – my friends and pupils. I wrote what it took to be a successful sniper: how he should be clad and equipped to keep him warm and make everything easy and convenient for him. I mentioned the special booklets of cards for keeping a tally of Nazi kills and the special passes for firing from beyond the usual range – giving permission to rove through all of the divisional sector when necessary. I mentioned the incorrect use of snipers in defence, which sometimes happened, and their effective use in battle.

When, in my view, the manuscript was ready, and had been discussed and approved in the ward, proof-read one final time by me and reworked, and then typed up, I telephoned one of the numbers given to me from the hospital director's office.

Two of us set off for the Smolny together. Major Pyotr Antonovich Glukhikh, who had been discharged from hospital by then, was summoned to escort me to the Political Section of the Leningrad Front. With his help at the Smolny we easily found the man the manuscript had to be handed over to. And only then did I sigh with relief, when I had passed it from my hands to his.

The same day in the same place, at the Political Section, I was presented with a new inscribed watch – an exact copy of the one found in my stomach, except that the inscription on the lid was different: 'From the Political Section of the Leningrad Front to Sniper Nikolaev'. Along with the watch I received an invitation to the first rally of front-line snipers at the Smolny.

# 11.

# The Snipers' Rally

On 22 February 1942, with my invitation in my pocket, I managed to walk by myself from the hospital to the Smolny. Our Lena had been ordered to escort me there on this occasion.

'You're still weak, and you could go astray on your own, and arrive late for all I know. And I know the city well and I'll take you there by the shortest route,' she said in a tone that brooked no protests. Lena's arguments were convincing, and her course of action was approved by our hospital ward and, the main thing, by the senior sister of the department, her mother, Alexandra Ivanovna.

Lena really did know the city very well. There was little time left till 1500 hours. We were hurrying; we had nothing to rely on but our own feet. Along the way we encountered trolley buses standing by the sides of the city's wide streets. Public transport in Leningrad was not operating; the electricity which powered the trolleybuses and trams before the war was no longer available.

However much we hurried, we only just got to the Smolny in time. Brave Lena wished me luck and immediately turned back; she had a long way to go. It was with a sinking feeling that I showed my invitation to the official on duty at the Smolny.

'Why are you late and why are you on your own?' he asked

sternly, looking at the invitation. 'And your papers?'

'I have no papers, just this . . . I'm from the hospital. I was invited by Comrade Zhdanov,' I tried to explain. 'You can telephone. They'll confirm it!' And I held out the list of telephone numbers written in Andrey Alexandrovich's own hand.

The official began to ring around and, to my delight, everything was cleared up very quickly – literally in a couple of minutes, I was handing my overcoat in at the cloakroom. After shedding my street clothes and tidying myself up in front of the huge mirror, I went up the stairs.

The corridor was deserted. Only very occasionally some soldiers who had been held up somewhere would run past me in tunics which smelled of the smoke of war and disappear behind the door of the chess hall. I felt uncomfortable before them in my spick and span new uniform, and I stood there looking around indecisively.

Then two more soldiers went past me in animated conversation, heading for the hall. One of them looked familiar.

'Yuri! Semyonov!' I cried out in desperation. 'Wait for me!'

They both stopped and looked in surprise in my direction, then came up closer, and Semyonov threw himself upon me.

'Yevgeni! Greetings! Where did you spring from?' And suddenly, without hearing my response, he dashed into the hall and vanished behind the door.

'What's the matter with him?' I asked the other soldier.

'I don't understand myself,' he replied.

We got talking. It turned out that he was a sniper from the 6th Regiment of our 21st Division. I found out that a big group of our fellows – about thirty of them – had come to the gathering. And he began to list familiar names. But he did not finish; out of the hall came a group of lads whom I recognised immediately.

Swiftly striding at the head of the group was Yuri Semyonov, and behind him, smiling, followed my true friends and comrades-in-arms – Ivan Dobrik, Ivan Karpov, Zagid Rakhmatullin, Sergei Korchagin, Alexei Shesterik and our other lads.

'Take a look. It really is our Yevgeni! You mean he's alive?' And Ivan Karpov squeezed me with all his strength.

'Nikolaev! How are you, old fellow?' said Dobrik in Ukrainian and gave me a hug.

After them the others began to squeeze me. They slapped me on the back, shoulders and arms as if they wanted to test my solidity, make sure I was alive.

'Come with us. We'll find a place for you,' said Yuri Semyonov and pulled me after him into the hall. The other lads followed us.

We were all in a state of great excitement both from the meeting and from the environment in which we found ourselves, being lads straight from the front line or from hospital. From the fact that we were now all in the Smolny.

I could not wait to find out how things were in the regiment, if my comrades were alive and well, what had our friends achieved, what was happening on the front line – but there was no time to talk. People in military and civilian dress were emerging from side doors and heading towards the presidium table.

'I won't be leaving you any more,' I managed to whisper.

'They won't let you out of hospital!'

'If they won't let me go nicely, I'll run away! I'll get better in the regiment!'

'Then come with us right away. We're on Liteiny Street, staying at Red Army House.'

As soon as the members of the Presidium had sat down at their table and the applause in the hall had died down, complete silence descended. Divisional Commissar Kuznetsov, a member of the Military Council of the Leningrad Front, had the floor. 'Comrades, tomorrow the whole country is marking the day of the Workers' and Peasants' Red Army [officially the 'Day of the Red Army and the Navy', celebrated annually on 23 February]. We are gathered with you to celebrate with the whole country this important day for our homeland . . .'

He did not speak for long – it was wartime! After talking briefly about the birth and the glorious military path of our army,

Kuznetsov noted its significance during the harsh times of the present day: a time of war against Nazism. Then he spoke about the formation of a sniper movement within the armies on our front for exterminating Nazis, about its necessity in a period of positional war against German invaders, and named the best of the best exterminators of the Nazi scum.

Andrey Alexandrovich Zhdanov, who followed him, called snipers the true heroes of the Great War for the Fatherland and called for the sniper movement to be greatly enlarged. 'We were pleased to report to the Central Committee of the Communist Party that, just within the first twenty days of January, delegates to this gathering and participants in wartime competition, our snipers, wiped out over 7,000 German troops and officers,' said Comrade Zhdanov. His words were greeted by a storm of applause. He went on:

> By a decree of the Presidium of the USSR Supreme Soviet dated 6 February 1942, the leading soldiers on our front have been awarded the exalted title of Hero of the Soviet Union. The names of Lieutenant Kozlov, Junior Lieutenant Yakovlyev, Sergeant-Major Vezhlivtsev, Sergeant Pchelintsev, Privates Golichenkov and Smolyachkov, Lieutenant Fomin, Deputy Political Adviser Kalinin, Senior Sergeant Loskutov and Senior Lieutenant Sinyavin are well known on our front.
>
> Lieutenant Nikolai Andreyevich Kozlov personally annihilated over 300 Nazi troops and officers. Mercilessly exterminating the Nazi scum because a sacred cause for Deputy Political Adviser Kalinin: 155 German invaders were wiped out by this celebrated member of the Leningrad Young Communist League, ardent Soviet patriot, and national hero. Communist Party member Sergeant Loskutov has earned eternal renown and the respect of the Soviet people by annihilating 117 Nazis, and Party member Senior Lieutenant Sinyavin

has dispatched 190 Nazi troops and officers to the next world.

The soldiers on our front must learn from our heroes the art of irresistibly striking at the enemy. The experience of the leading snipers must be made accessible to all soldiers at the front, in order to develop thousands of new masters of marksmanship. The objective now is to move from individual snipers to the formation of detachments, platoons and companies of snipers. All troops, officers and political advisers of the front must come to grips with this responsible and honoured task.

May the award with which our finest military comrades have been presented inspire us all to new feats. May the glory of Soviet arms grow. May the ranks of the heroes of the Soviet land multiply!

Comrade Zhdanov finished, to thunderous applause. Then began the presentation of awards to the heroes who had been named.

First to be called was the name of sniper Feodosy Smolyachkov, to whom this high honour was awarded posthumously: Feodosy Artemyevich Smolyachkov, sniper of the 13th Rifle Division, who had wiped out 125 Nazis with 126 bullets but perished on 15 January 1942. Our heroes went up to the top table and Comrade Zhdanov presented the awards personally. He also pinned the Gold Star of 'Hero of the Soviet Union' and the Order of Lenin onto their tunics – for each of them. Among those who received this exalted title was my fellow-townsman, Vladimir Pchelintsev, who had wiped out 102 Nazis. Sniper Vezhlivtsev had accounted for 134 of them and Golichenkov for 140. The chief of the front's general staff, Major General Gusev, rose and solemnly, with long pauses after every word, proceeded to read a command to the troops of the Leningrad Front. 'On behalf of the Presidium of the USSR Supreme Soviet, in recognition of the initiative shown in launching military competition for extermination of the German invaders, the exemplary fulfilment of commissions to destroy enemy personnel and machinery, and the valour and courage demonstrated in the course of this ... I award!' he singled out this verb, made a big pause, looked out into the hall and, after this, loudly announced, 'the Order of Lenin – to Deputy Political Adviser Babin, Alexander Vladimirovich.'

The deputy head of the Front's general staff held out a little red casket and an equally red booklet to Comrade Zhdanov, who had been standing there all this time between the presidium table and the rostrum. Andrey Alexandrovich looked out into the hall and said, 'I call on Comrade Babin to come up for the presentation.'

Alexander Babin climbed up onto the stage and walked up to Comrade Zhdanov, shook the hand extended to him, and with his other hand took the red casket from Andrey Alexandrovich's hands. The, turning to the audience, he loudly and distinctly pronounced the words: 'I serve the Soviet Union!' The hall exploded in applause.

Following Babin the other named recipients proceeded to walk up to the presidium table one by one in alphabetical order. In ninth place was our Tambov Young Communist League representative, Yuri Semyonov. All in all, we counted twelve people awarded the Order of Lenin. Five of them were soldiers of our 21st Division.

'Order of the Red Banner!' the general once again solemnly proclaimed and began to name the recipients. They got up from their seats and headed for the table, red in the face from agitation and embarrassment.

But not all of them went up to the presidium table; many of them were still being treated for wounds. Vladimir Dudin, our sergeant-major and sniper, had the Order of the Red Banner presented to him in his hospital ward on the very same day. Others had perished, knowing neither of this solemn occasion or their own award.

And now the Order of the Red Banner was presented to Ivan Dobrik, while Ivan Karpov also emerged with the same award.

I congratulated my friends and helped them to attach the orders to their tunics.

Then I suddenly heard the announcement: 'Order of the Red Banner . . . Nikolaev, Yevgeni Adrianovich!'

I sat as if I were tied to the chair, unable to bring myself to get up. 'What if it's not me. Imagine the embarrassment if two Nikolaevs get up.'

'Go on! What are you still sitting there for? You've been called up,' Ivan Karpov whispered to me.

Completely at a loss, I got up from my seat and headed down the broad aisle to the table.

'Is Nikolaev present?' said Comrade Zhdanov with a smile, held out the box containing the order and shook my hand.

Without letting my hand go, he said, turning to the audience:

'Comrade Nikolaev has come to us from hospital. Let's wish him a speedy recovery! And that after he gets out of hospital he will knock out the Nazis as well has he did before he was wounded. I congratulate you, Comrade Nikolaev, on your award.'

'I serve the Soviet Union!' I replied in a loud voice to the applause of those sitting in the hall. And softly, just to Comrade Zhdanov, I said: 'Thank you, Andrey Alexandrovich!'

The audience applauded. Comrade Zhdanov again shook my hand and then said, for my ears only: 'Isn't there anything you want to say?'

'I do, Andrey Alexandrovich!'

He raised his hand in a bid for calm. As soon as silence descended in the hall, Andrey Alexandrovich said: 'Attention, please! Sniper Nikolaev wishes to say a few words!' And he nodded to me and beckoned towards the rostrum with his eyes.

In a state of agitation, I approached the rostrum and stopped beside it. I was afraid I would disappear behind it, as it seemed too big for me. I had a lot of thoughts in my head, and nice, warm words I wanted to say, but felt that I might lose my way from the agitation gripping me and, since it was not possible to talk for long, I decided to keep it as brief as possible. I stood for a little with my eyes closed, thought about it, calmed down a bit, and the words I needed came of their own accord.

> Comrades! Thank you to the Party and the government for this high honour. I will do my best to deserve it. I swear that, as long as my heart still beats, as long as my eyes can see, and my hands can firmly grip a rifle, I will fight the Nazi pestilence. I have killed 76 Nazis. That's not many. I promise to wipe out 300 of them! And I will do it. And I will teach my young comrades how to do it.

'Well done, well spoken,' Comrade Zhdanov laughed. 'Brief and clear! Well done!'

Happy that I had not gone awry and had said exactly what I felt, what I thought and wanted to say, I returned to my seat to the applause of the presidium and then of the entire audience. My friends were waiting for me. Ivan Dobrik shook my hand along the way and several other pairs of hands were extended, even from strangers, while Ivan Karpov was already taking the gleaming gold and red and white enamel order out of the box and pinning it on my chest.

While we were congratulating one another and examining and attaching the decorations to tunics, the presidium announced: 'Comrades! Our gathering will continue following a break of one hour in the Kirov Red Army House, to which participants are to make their own way.'

In under an hour we were already in the Red Army House on Liteiny Street. As we walked through the city it seemed that the whole of Leningrad was looking at us today and seeing the decorations through our overcoats.

'Tidy yourselves up and clean your boots – and then go straight into the hall! The session is in fifteen minutes!' announced the senior officer in the dormitory.

In the big room partitioned off for our division there were about twenty beds pushed together. Lying on them were some paper bags.

'Well, Yevgeni, make yourself at home. This bed here's free,' the lads told me. 'We'll spend the night here and the day after tomorrow you can come straight to the regiment with us!'

'Agreed! Only tomorrow I will drop in at the hospital for a minute. I've got some stuff left there and I have to say goodbye to folk.'

'Go, of course. Show them your order! Well, let's go. We're being called already.'

'Just a minute, let's have a look what kind of bags they have left us.'

They turned out to be gifts sent in to the soldiers of the Leningrad Front from unoccupied territory. I looked at mine. The first thing that caught my eye was a letter all mottled with indecipherable signatures at the end. As far as I could gather, the letter was written by the staff of some Party district committee. It was they who had put a parcel together, congratulated me and all other soldiers on the special day and wished us a speedy victory.

It was a pity they had not left their address and I could not thank them.

In a box lay five packets of 'White Sea Canal' brand cigarettes, two books, some woollen socks and gloves of the same material, while wrapped up in paper were some nuts, a few spiced honey-cakes and some chocolates. But the dearest item to me was the present from the children of the kindergarten – a huge handkerchief with a red fringe. In its four corners were inscribed the names: Olga, Vasya, Lida and Vlad. And in the middle were the words 'A Presint'. The misspelling was particularly touching.

'Time to go, lads! Conclude your meeting with unoccupied territory!' said the senior officer, and we regretfully put away our paper bags.

Music thundered and, to the sounds of a brass band, which we had not heard for a long time, the guests mounted the broad marble staircase and proceeded into the spacious foyer. There a concert was being presented by the front-line song and dance ensemble of the Kirov Red Army House.

Among the performers, who had been recruited from front-line units, I spotted some of our own, who had been transferred here from our divisional ensemble. Performing in the front-line ensemble was our 'prima donna', Valya Kaikova with her friend, and other lads and lasses with whom I was very friendly. The head of our club was a smart chap, Political Adviser Alexander Danilovich Cherkassov, with whom I, as a former theatre member, had things to talk about when time allowed.

On the wall of the broad corridor were a number of portraits, over which we saw the inscription 'Leading snipers of the Leningrad Front'. Among them was my photograph, showing me with a machine gun in my hands. 'When did they photograph me? And why with a machine gun? It must have been when I was in reconnaissance!' I guessed. Beside my portrait was one of Ivan Dobrik. Under the portraits were long inscriptions. On myself I read: 'Y. A. Nikolaev – senior sergeant. Secretary of the Young Communist League committee, bold and full of initiative as a sniper and scout. Penetrated many times into the enemy dispositions and fulfilled difficult commissions from his superiors. In the course of just one day wiped out eleven Nazi pillagers. In all Comrade Nikolaev has exterminated seventy-six German lowlife.'

We realised that the Front command and the organisers of the gathering had decided to arrange as many pleasant surprises as possible. It was announced to us that there would now be a performance from a celebrated cabaret singer whose repertoire was known and sung by the entire Soviet Union. It was Klavdia Ivanovna Shulzhenko and her jazz band. Like many theatrical and cabaret performers, she had remained in besieged Leningrad and gave concerts for the population of the city and the front-line units.

The band was conducted by Klavdia Ivanovna's husband, Vladimir Koralli, a likeable man of above average height and quite plump, a congenial sort of fellow, wearing a military uniform with no badges of rank and a small Browning pistol at his side.

Klavdia Ivanovna sang several well-known songs that were everyone's favourites as well as a couple of new ones which had only just been created in besieged Leningrad. And she repeated every song twice, in response to calls for an encore. We would not have let her off the stage if the conductor, Vladimir Koralli, had not announced: 'Don't worry, comrades! Klavdia Ivanovna will sing some more, I give you my firm promise. But in the meantime you are invited into other premises, where we will continue our festive evening.' Everyone rose regretfully and went into the 'other premises'.

On the way we, the group from the 21st Division, were apprehended 'for a minute' and invited into one of the other halls. There we were lined up and a command was read out: 'The Political Department of the Leningrad Front awards military weaponry, inscribed snipers' rifles, to Comrades . . .' And we, snipers Dobrik, Karpov, Rakhmatullin and I, were presented with inscribed snipers' rifles with a metal plate on the butt and an engraved inscription. I read the one on my rifle: 'Presented to Nazi exterminator, sniper Nikolaev, Y. A., from the Political Department of the Leningrad Front, 22.2.42'.

'We serve the Soviet Union!' we responded in chorus to the greeting of the Political Department representative. Kneeling down and holding the rifles with our arms outstretched, we kissed them and swore that from these weapons we would target the Nazis accurately and in large numbers – until complete victory over the hated enemy was achieved.

Excited by what we had just experienced, we headed for the mysterious 'other premises'. They turned out to be a huge hall where music was thundering out.

'Comrades, you are invited to the table!'

Indeed, to hear such a phrase during the siege was something you could only dream of. In the large hall, from wall to wall, long tables had been set out in the shape of a trident and covered with snow-white tablecloths. And on the tables! Plates of real red beet, cabbage and potato salad at two or three spoonfuls per head. Two slices of bread spread with sprats and black caviar. Bread, chocolates, cigarettes, bottles of vodka, beer and lemonade –

double the official rations for each of us. All this was neatly set out and superbly served.

When we had all taken our seats, it turned out that I was sitting at one of the corners – I could see not only our entire team, but also those who were sitting at the table which formed the base of the trident: the Front command, our new heroes and Klavdia Ivanovna Shulzhenko. Almost side by side with Shulzhenko sat an embarrassed Vladimir Pchelintsev, who was still adjusting to his new title as Hero of the Soviet Union.

When complete silence had descended in the hall, the officer in command rose from his seat.

> Comrades! Today we have a double celebration: we are marking the anniversary of the Red Army with the whole country and we are honouring our heroes – our Nazi exterminators. And I can appreciate your surprise when you look at these festively covered tables. This is a gift to you, defenders of Leningrad, from unoccupied territory. The homeland is not forgetting us! So let us raise our glasses and drink to our beloved homeland, to the Communist Party, our heroic people and to the victory which is bound to come.

Everyone rose to their feet and a harmonious 'Hurrah!' rang out. And then there were more toasts, more speeches, and then toasts again, although everything had long been drunk and the plates were now empty.

Choosing a convenient moment, Vladimir Pchelintsev rose from his seat, turned to Shulzhenko and said: 'Klavdia Ivanovna, you promised to sing for us. If, of course, you are not too tired . . .'

'How can one not sing for heroes? Let's have some music, Vlad!' Klavdia Ivanovna immediately responded.

The band began to play and the singer sang her celebrated number 'The Blue Headscarf'. And then there were more and more songs. She sang as we had never heard before.

Emboldened, I also made a request of Shulzhenko.

'Klavdia Ivanovna, you have sung almost everything but my favourite song. Could you please sing 'Mother'?

And the sounds of the song, so heartfelt and tender, descended over the hushed hall.

'Mother . . . no words are brighter and dearer . . .'

Many had tears in their eyes. Not only for me but for others it apparently conjured up thoughts of home, mothers, family, children – of precious peace-time years.

When the last notes had died away and the song was over, the thunderous applause shook the whole building and did not die down for a long time. And we, the youngsters, twenty-year-olds, recalled the loved ones who were patiently waiting for us to come following victory.

As if she had divined our mood, Klavdia Ivanovna began to sing:

> No, it's not your eyes
> I'll remember at the hour of parting.
> It's not your voice
> I will hear in the silence.
> It's those tender, trembling hands
> That I'll remember
> And they will remind me
> Of you . . .

We sat deep into the night, singing and talking. Everyone had cherished memories of his own, and related or listened to what was dearest to, or beloved of, each of us.

I sat at a table with a musician from the Front ensemble band, whom I had just got to know. It turned out he was from Tambov. We remembered the streets or our home town and discovered acquaintances in common.

'Well, who is it reminiscing about Tambov? Let me look at him!' said a voice behind me.

I looked around. Before me stood Vladimir Pchelintsev. Swaying gently on his chest was the gleaming Golden Star of a Hero of the Soviet Union. We got talking. And Vladimir Pchelintsev told me a lot about himself. He had been born in Tambov in 1919. A year later he had lost his father – he had died defending the young Soviet republic. Vladimir's stepfather was a military man. Moscow, Yaroslavl, Petrozavodsk, Leningrad – the family spent time in a number of cities while Vladimir was growing up. Vladimir was a lively and sociable lad. He loved active games and was fascinated by the books of Thomas Mayne Reid, Walter Scott, and Jules Verne. He liked Pioneer camps with their spartan mode of life, hiking, wargames and camp fires.

Vladimir was attracted to shooting from his earliest years. While still a boy, in 1935, he achieved the standard for the Voroshilov Marksman badge. And in 1937 he headed the school team at the national shooting championships and won first place. His prize was a TOZ-9 small-bore rifle.

He was fascinated not only by shooting. At his institute he played soccer and volleyball, loved tennis and took part in track and field athletics. While still a student he graduated from sniper school and trained for the title 'USSR Master of Sport', but 22 June 1941 put an end to all his plans. A student in his third year, he put his textbooks aside and took up a military rifle. True, he was turned down by the recruitment office, when he appeared on the very first day of the war. Vladimir then set off to construct defence works. Soon they began to recruit volunteers to combat enemy parachute drops and Vladimir was enrolled in the 83rd 'Search and Destroy' Battalion. Vladimir Pchelintsev became a sniper and observer. His tally of vengeance on the enemy rose day by day: twenty-five, then thirty-six and sixty Nazis were wiped out by his accurate shooting. He received his first award – a watch engraved with his name.

Day and night, in freezing cold and rain, Vladimir patiently sought out the enemy. At night he set up marksman's foxholes and camouflage, while during the day he engaged in observation. To make the foxhole clean and comfortable he furnished it with mats made from woven twigs. On the parapet he would set up forks for his rifle so that his arms would not get so tired. He would study the enemy defences thoroughly down to the smallest details; not a single metre must remain unexamined. 'To see everything while remaining unseen' – such was his motto.

As an experienced search-and-destroy soldier, he knew that the enemy was cunning, clever and insidious. Pchelintsev had seen all this at close quarters. And to preserve his own life he had to be cleverer, more cunning and nimble – stronger than the enemy. In winter Vladimir would pour water on the snow in front of his gun-port, so that it would not puff up when he fired and give his position away. He hung the gun-port with cheesecloth, so that it blended with the snow. He could see everything, but his opponents could not. Vladimir knew from the newspapers that other snipers were operating beside him and they had their own tally of vengeance, their own experience. He began to correspond with them and the snipers established a real military liaison and began to compete with one another.

The past day had been a joyful and memorable one for Vladimir. He had also received an inscribed sniper's rifle and on the butt of it sparkled a metal plate reading: 'To Nazi exterminator, sniper V. Pchelintsev from the Political Department of the Leningrad Front'. We sat till late, deep in conversation. And none of us knew back then that no more than six months later, Vladimir Pchelintsev would travel with Hero of the Soviet Union, the Sevastopol sniper Lyudmila Pavlichenko, and Nikolai Krasavchenko as part of the Soviet youth delegation to an international student congress in the United States of America. Along with them he would visit Iraq, Egypt, Central Africa and Britain. He would feast his eyes on jungles and deserts, on the blue of the unknown southern seas, and experience London's famous fogs . . .

# 12.

# Back in the Regiment

Only three days had passed since the front-line gathering, but Comrade Zhdanov's call: 'To ensure that the destruction of the Nazi plague becomes a matter of honour for every soldier and officer on the Leningrad Front' had already, judging by the newspapers, been taken up by all units on the front. It was felt in our division.

The destruction of the Nazis had become a mass cause. With every passing day it assumed greater and greater proportions. More and more detachments appeared calling themselves snipers.

The regimental commander, by now Colonel Rodionov, was in his dugout with his deputy for political affairs, Senior Battalion Commissar Agashin.

'Comrade Colonel!' I addressed Rodionov on entering the dugout, 'Permission to report: Senior Sergeant Nikolaev returned from hospital for further service.'

'At last! Well, greetings!' and the colonel extended his hand. 'You're back just in time. We have a lot of work on at the moment and not enough people.'

'Well, tell us all about it,' said Agashin. 'Did they sew you together again? What's your health like?'

'Thank you, Comrade Senior Battalion Commissar, I feel fine and I can't complain about my health.'

'Well, show the colonel and me your documents – the hospital certification. Have you got them with you?'

'As it happens, Comrade Commissar, they didn't give me any. Why would I need them if I'm well again? But if they're really needed, they'll send them on, I think? Their actual words were: "Well, you're well again, Nikolaev, you can go back to the regiment." So here I am . . .'

'You're taking us for a ride, mate! And you're not quite well. You've run away from hospital, without any documents – you can't fool me!' said Agashin with a smile. 'But as to your love for the regiment, and dashing back here rather than into the rear, thank you for that. Well, where are we going to put him, Comrade Colonel?'

'What do you mean, where? Where he's supposed to be. What we need is a live soldier, a healthy one!' said Rodionov emphatically. 'I order you straight to the medical section, to Polikarpov, to recover. Three weeks of rest and treatment in the medical section, and then we'll see!'

'But you yourself, where would you like to go? Political work or military service?'

'I'm a soldier, Comrade Commissar. I'll go wherever you command. But I have to target the Germans – I gave my word! I made a promise to Comrade Zhdanov at the snipers' rally.'

'I know. I've heard. You gave your word to wipe out 300 Nazis. Keep your word. But we've given you a new title – Deputy Regimental Political Adviser. So add a star to your sleeve and a fourth triangle to your collar-tab.'

I was warmly welcomed in the medical section by my fellow townsmen and friends. First of all, they fed me, and late at night, when all the talking was done, we lay down to sleep on some semi-soft plank bunks which stretched along the whole wall of what had formerly been the cellar of a school.

During the day the medical section was empty. Only the doctors and sisters on duty remained. The lads were distributed among the regiments. Each of them was doing good work of his own. Only I was idle; I made up for lost sleep and food and read voraciously. I read everything that came to hand – from various medical guides to school textbooks. Apart from me there were only a few lying in the medical section at that time; the division was not in any active engagements at the time.

In the evenings, when our 'family' gathered again in the spacious premises, we sang songs, had heart to heart talks and even danced. We were especially fond of listening to Military Assistant Ivan Mikhailovich Vasilyev. He had a remarkable voice and knew many fine songs, but the songs that had emerged from the war were particularly popular. Those able to do so sang along with him, but usually he sang solo to the accompaniment of an accordion played in virtuoso style by Medical Assistant Ivan Matuzko.

But however good it was with friends in the medical section, my heart yearned for the front line, for real work. A week later, without waiting for the prescribed period, I convinced the head of the section, Major Polikarpov, to let me go back to the regiment. The same day I found myself in the 1st Company and taking on my new responsibility – a rifle platoon.

The company commander was a native of Tambov. Senior Lieutenant Pyotr Andreyevich Shilov had been called up from reserve back during the Soviet–Finnish War, and had remained in the forces of the NKVD. The garrison which he commanded was protecting the railway bridge across the Sestra river on the Karelian Isthmus. That was where Pyotr Andreyevich was when the Great War for the Fatherland started. A man of rare courage, fair and calm in service, Shilov was liked by the troops and was on good terms with those in command over him. The political adviser in the company was Senior Lieutenant Lapko, one of the early Party recruits and a representative of the Kirov works, an intelligent and daring officer. My deputy platoon commander was a lad from Leninakan, Sergo Kazarian, who was also a sniper and a good trainer.

Through our joint efforts Sergo Kazarian and I quickly put our second platoon in order. We began by deepening and strengthening the trenches and then refitting all the firing positions and dugouts. Additional foxholes were dug and ammunition stores, toilet facilities and even our own bath-house were set up. In a word, I took over troops who had been stuck in defensive positions, shook them up a bit and began gradually to prepare them to attack.

This meant starting with their outward appearance. As soon as we had finished the earthworks, I ordered them all to clean their uniforms, have a good wash themselves and only to go around with clean collars. These measures raised morale among my subordinates; it became more pleasant for them to look at one another. Neat and tidy, with their hair cut, and their belts tight around their waists, they now looked like soldiers from the pre-war period. Our platoon and the defences we occupied came to set an example, first within the company and then within the battalion. Our practices were praised by the regimental command, who often visited the front line.

And only when they had been through this 'reform' and felt its impact personally did the troops realise that it was not just carried out to gain praise from their superiors. Individuals of the nine fraternal republics of the Soviet Union became friends, became even more strongly united, got to know one another well, and were ready to fulfil any assignment. I had confidence in my troops and they believed in their young commander. And so began my new life in the regiment.

It was difficult, but I found time to go out 'hunting' for Nazis with my sniper's rifle, more and more stars appeared on its butt, and my tally of exterminated Nazis grew. I also trained many of my troops in the sniper's art. I was assisted in this by my deputy, Sergo Kazarian, and by Sergeant Ivan Karpov, commander of a machine-gun platoon.

After forty years and more, even today I can still visualise each of my soldiers. Take the sturdy, nimble and assiduous Ukrainian Roman Stepanovich Moskovko. He was my rock, fulfilling the functions of platoon commandant. With his large miner's hands, Moskovko loved to get stuck in with a sapper's shovel. So, the communication routes and firing positions in the platoon's defences were always in an exemplary condition. Roman Stepanovich was not afraid of work, always found something to do, and handled it superbly. He constantly dug out trenches collapsed by enemy fire, ensured they remained clear and improved the firing positions, bringing up whole cubic metres of earth to the surface by night. He was like this in clashes with the Nazis – calculating, balanced, calm and, at the same time, possessed of a certain fury.

Private Samuil Davidovich Blyakher had been in the home guard. Of amazingly short stature, he was a frail and puny Odessa Jew. He loved to talk. In his free time he would endlessly show photos of his family and boast about them: 'Right here, in the middle – that's me and my Roza. And the kiddies.' Anyone looking at the photograph would be faced by the enormous, big-breasted, buxom Roza, who towered over her husband. And at their parents' feet and to the side – a host of scruffy children. Blyakher had still not worked out how many children he had left at home – eleven or a full dozen. According to Samuil Davidovich, who possessed that celebrated Odessan sense of humour, his wife Roza, a domineering, but kind and cheerful, woman, would look at the children and often joke to her husband: 'Well, what shall we do, Samuil – clean this lot up or make some more?'

A frequent visitor to our platoon was Zagid Kalievich Rakhmatullin, a sniper well known in the division and a soldier of the 4th Company. No longer a young man, he was of short stature and had a broad face with black, slightly slanted eyes. He would call in on us on his way – either to go out 'hunting' or on his return – to chat with those from his own part of the country. 'Krupno govoryat za zhizn' ('Much talk about life'), our Odessan native Blyakher would say back then. Zagid often served me as an interpreter – from Kazakh, Tatar and Uzbek into Russian, and vice versa.

There was nobody in the army who was not familiar with the division's best snipers, at least by name. And that was under-standable; at that time their names were never out of the divisional newspaper. A Communist Party member for some years and a sniper who had wiped out over a hundred Nazis, Zagid Rakhmatullin was well known to everyone in the platoon. He carried great authority. During lulls in action the troops would ask Zagid to talk about himself. Then, fraternally sharing his Morshansk tobacco from an embroidered pouch, he would tell us about his family, his collective farm, peacetime life, and his achievements at the front. And he knew how to tell a story.

Zagid was born in 1913 in the village of Mukhomedyarovo, in the Suvandyk district of Orenburg Region. His family were poor peasants. Zagid lost his father in 1921 – he died of hunger, leaving the boy along with his sick mother. The young lad had to work as a day labourer for a local moneybags. And when collectivisation was announced in 1929, as a labourer he was the first to be accepted into the collective farm. And in the Young Communist League at the same time. In 1930 the bright and industrious lad went on a course for tractor drivers. Until 1939 Rakhmatullin worked as a tractor driver on his collective farm and won distinction as a Stakhanovite for high productivity. In 1937 he had been accepted into the Party. He took part in the Soviet–Finnish War and fought the Nazis from the very first days of the Great War for the Fatherland. When the locals saw him off to the front, the secretary of the Party's district committee told Zagid: 'Make sure you're a top-class soldier, just as you were a top-class grain farmer.' And in front of everybody Zagid promised to justify the faith of his fellow-villagers and swore than he would heroically defend his homeland.

On arrival at his unit, the 21st NKVD Division near Leningrad, Zagid began from his very first days keenly studying warfare and military technology and mastering the sniper's art. He had a powerful desire to wipe out as many Nazis as possible. As a Communist, he realised that his place was there, on the front line, where the going was tough. And he became a real exterminator of the Nazi vermin. He gave his word that he would wipe out at least a hundred of them.

When Zagid went out 'hunting' for the first time, he did not lose his presence of mind: with some accurate shots he took out an enemy officer and four soldiers at the same time. The Nazis discovered the spot from where the successful sniper was directing his lethal fire and carpeted it with mortar bombs. But Zagid remained calm; he was cleverly camouflaged and safely protected from the shell fragments.

On the Leningrad Front fate brought him together with people like himself – strong and determined lads. Their big hands had once been accustomed to holding the wheel of a tractor, combine harvester or cotton-picking machine. They were well used to carefully picking up boxes of 'white gold' and tenderly letting the golden grains of wheat pour from their hands. Nobody had taught them the science of killing. But the soldiers matured, became hardened in battle.

At the beginning of April 1943 Zagid wrote his family a letter in which he said:

> Don't be concerned on my behalf. I have kept my word: 148 Nazis wiped out by my sniper's rifle. I have been awarded the Order of the Red Star. Comrade Zhdanov thanked me personally for my achievements. I have given my word to raise my tally of exterminated Nazis to 200 and I will keep it. Keep working calmly, my dear ones, for the good of our motherland; we shall rout the Nazis.

And indeed, when I met Rakhmatullin in 1944 in our divisional medical section, he told me: 'They've started keeping snipers' records. They weren't around in your time.' And he showed me a 'Personal Record of Nazi Kills'. On the opposite page were graphs showing the total number of Nazis in a day and the growing tally. According to Zagid's record, he had reached 177.

Zagid fought superbly. Whatever he did, he did thoroughly and reliably. I recall his clashes with Ivan Dobrik, who, according to Rakhmatullin recklessly 'asked for trouble and fought like a lion'. Zagid always strove to be side by side with his friend. In the intervals between engagements, he told Dobrik: 'You're a daring fighter, Ivan. Boldness is a good thing. But it's not worth losing your head; it may come in useful!' Ivan frowned in response and, interrupting Zagid, declared impatiently in Ukrainian: 'I can't do otherwise, friend, you know that! You've got your folk at home but mine are under the Nazis! I'm mad at the Nazis . . .'

One time the commander of Rakhmatullin's 4th Company was seriously wounded in battle. Zagid loaded him on his back and dragged him towards their trenches. The Germans had resolved to take both of them prisoner and charged towards them. Then Zagid laid the commander on the grass and began to fight off the Nazis with grenades, and then to target them with his sniper's rifle. And, having beaten them off, he continued on his way, hauling his commander after him. Having got there, he took him to the medical section and immediately went back to the trenches, and again dashed into battle.

One day Zagid was escorting a Nazi major whom he had personally taken prisoner. A motorcyclist stopped by him along the way.

'Where are you taking him?' asked the captain on the motorbike, his eyes darting warily from side to side.

'I'm taking a prisoner to the divisional staff,' Zagid answered.

'Well, I've been looking for him . . . so, go back, soldier and I'll take the prisoner myself – I came specially for him.'

'No, I'm not giving the prisoner up. I have been ordered to deliver him and I'll do it myself.'

'Quiet! I order you to hand the prisoner over, or else I'll shoot you for not obeying an order!'

'But I don't know you!' replied Zagid, feeling that something was not quite right. And, just in case, he placed his own rifle at the ready.

Zagid nevertheless handed over the prisoner to the captain; he was accustomed to obeying officers. But when he returned to the regiment and reported what had happened, his own commander swore he would shoot Zagid for not carrying out his order. The sniper was bailed out by regimental counter-reconnaissance, which had caught both of them – the 'captain', who turned out to be a Nazi dressed in our uniform, and the captured major.

Wounded several times at the front, Rakhmatullin returned to his collective farm a war invalid, where he re-joined the tractor brigade. His military decorations were complemented by a medal for peacetime labour. From 1945 to 1958 he was elected as a deputy to the Ziyanchurin Rural Council and he was a people's assessor in the district court. I once read a testimonial to Zagid presented on some occasion: 'A good family man, caring father, conscientious worker, supportive comrade, humble and always ready to offer help to anyone in need of it. His children are most disciplined and won top places in both their studies and work.' Could it be otherwise?

For every soldier battles are played out within the context of his own bounds, his own settings. In the case of Platoon Deputy Commander Sergo Kazarian these amounted to eighty-nine Nazis whom he wiped out with his sniper's rifle over a short period of time, repeated raids into the enemy rear, and continual fighting and serious wounds. One of his tussles on the southern slopes of the Pulkovo Heights, which blocked the Nazis' path to Leningrad, also turned out to be a boundary line for Communist Sergo Kazarian.

The 2nd Platoon was advancing. Having stood in for his wounded platoon commander, Red Army Private Sergo Kazarian was observing nervously how precisely his orders were being carried out, how well the troops, covering one another, were dashing from cover to cover as they drew nearer to the enemy trenches. The 1st and 3rd Platoons, which were attacking from the flanks and were behind the 2nd, had fallen back. The Germans had managed to surround Kazarian's platoon and trap it in a ring of fire.

'Dig in!' Kazarian ordered his troops and was the first to get stuck in with his sapper's shovel. Now the Nazis were unable to target their fire, but they still managed to knock out a number of men.

'What should we do?' Sergo wondered. Ideas quickly darted through his mind, one after another, and he boldly decided to enter into 'do or die' combat with the enemy's numerous ranks.

'Make sure you're all taking adequate cover! Only fire single shots and only then when you're certain of a hit. Economise on cartridges!' the temporary commander's order went along the lines.

The Germans were amazed; a group of Soviet troops within a ring of fire not only failed to surrender but entered into unequal combat with them.

A German sniper looked up out of the trench. Kazarian aimed his machine gun at him and fired. The Nazi fell. Dispatch-rider Nemin wiped out a second Nazi. The Nazis then leapt out of their trenches and, pouring lead from their submachine guns, charged shouting at the daredevils with the intention of capturing them or finishing them off to the last man. But the machine-gun fire from our side intensified. Grenades were hurled at the Nazis. The Germans were forced to retreat. And then a hail of mortar fire descended on the sector occupied by the now blood-soaked platoon. Again they tried to attack our daredevils, but this time they were confronted by coordinated machine-gun fire from our troops.

'Russky, surrender!' cried the Nazis, no longer raising their heads above the parapets.

'Keep quiet and don't move!' Kazarian ordered his troops and continued cautiously watching the enemy trenches.

The Germans tried a different manoeuvre; they stationed machine gunners at the front and sent snipers to the flanks.

'Lie flat and don't raise your heads!' Kazarian ordered. 'We'll fight to the last cartridge! Leave the grenades in reserve! Let the Germans fire back in the meantime.'

The fighting did not let up for a moment. The Nazi snipers and machine gunners changed positions, striving to break the resistance of the gallant soldiers, but their efforts were in vain.

And so the day passed. A moonlit night fell. At midnight the platoon commander ordered Despatch Rider Nyemin to break through to our forces whatever the cost and try to bring up reinforcements. Nyemin had only crawled about three metres from their positions before the Germans spotted him. And again the mortar bombs started whining. They were exploding right beside them. Nyemin was wounded and the commander of the detachment, Kurmambekov was seriously wounded. Kazarian himself was hit in the shoulder. Without paying attention to his wound, Kazarian crept out and bandaged Nyemin's head. Kurmambekov was groaning softly.

The Germans decided that, after such massed fire, the Soviet troops would no longer resist. Again they came out of their trench and crawled towards the groaning Kurmambekov, who was lying not far from an earth and timber pillbox.

'No, you bastards! I won't let you have him!' whispered Sergo. He grabbed his machine gun, but saw that it had been damaged by a mortar fragment. Then Kazarian rose and threw three grenades, one after another, at the advancing Germans. One of the Nazis was killed, two were wounded, and the rest returned to their start line.

At this time a German sniper began firing at Kazarian. The first bullet tore through the kitbag on the commander's back. Sergo began to dig even deeper into the ground. But the bullets continued to whistle over him. Four bullets hit the kitbag and shot through his mess tin, but did not touch the commander. He froze to the spot . . . The German sniper decided that the Soviet soldier was dead. After firing several more shots, he fell silent. Kazarian was silent too and not moving.

Late at night Nyemin lapsed into semi-consciousness, became delirious and began loudly crying out and thrashing around. The German machine gunners directed their fire towards the sound of his voice. One of their rounds hit the wounded despatch rider. He died without regaining consciousness. Kazarian crept up to him, kissed his friend's parched lips, closed his eyes and whispered: 'Good-bye, comrade! We'll fight on and avenge you. I will not surrender any soldier, dead or alive, to Nazi desecration. And we will hold our line!'

Clouds appeared in the sky. They formed a cluster and blotted out the bright moon. Under cover of night a despatch rider from the company commander finally crept up to Kazarian.

'And we were already thinking you were dead,' he said.

'We're holding on, as you can see. Go back and tell the company commander to send up some men,' Kazarian asked. 'We won't leave our position! And the fascist scum can be driven out of their trench.' After half an hour reinforcements arrived. With a rapid attack the same night our troops drove the enemy out of their trenches and the position was firmly held.

Kazarian received nine wounds in the course of the war. 'I've got a strong heart, very strong!' he said with a joyful smile on his return to the regiment from hospital. 'It's made of Armenian granite!'

Gleaming on Sergo's breast were the Order of the Red Banner, the medal 'For Valour', and other decorations. At the first front-line snipers' rally he was also presented with an inscribed sniper's rifle.

Such was my deputy platoon commander.

Now a war invalid, Sergo Kazarian continued to work. He lived on Cosmonaut Avenue, Leningrad. He worked for many years as head of the mechanical and repair workshop of the No. 3 Fish-Processing Works. For several years in a row his workmates chose Communist Party member Kazarian as their team leader. He was secretary of the Party bureau.

# 13.

# An 'Invitation'

A sniper is certainly not only just a highly accurate marksman who fires from convenient positions hidden from the enemy. A Nazi-killer operates from time to time in the most inconceivable conditions. He sits in no man's land in ambush, isolated from the front line and from comrades able to help him. In such situations he remains at one with himself. He must know how to operate in any weather, winter and summer, in heat and cold, day and night. Alone, he must set up a reliable firing position close to the enemy front line or even actually in territory occupied by the Nazis. Moreover, there is nobody to check if you have camouflaged yourself well enough and how your firing position looks from the enemy's viewpoint.

It is good when snipers operate in pairs; that makes things significantly easier for them. But, as a rule, in my view, a good hunter of the Nazi beast goes out alone.

The difficult job of a sniper is equally dangerous in winter and summer. And it seems that everything unfortunate that can occur at the front has been created especially for him. Life is fine for a marksman who is firing from his own front line, from concealed firing positions. Whatever goes wrong, his mates will always help. He can move around constantly in his hidden lair, changing his position. And he sees the enemy only from one viewpoint – straight ahead.

A sniper has many enemies. Especially in summer. Apart from the main one – the enemy – there are others from whom you never know what to expect. They can be bees, wasps, flies, ants and even field mice . . .

I remember once on a fine summer's day Ivan Dobrik and I were lying in ambush. We had to lie out in no man's land, in thick grass, in a flat, open area – almost right under the enemy's noses. We conducted observations of the German front line and the approaches to it, having correctly calculated that, in thick grass in a flat field without a single landmark, it would be difficult for the Nazis to spot us.

We would have lain there calmly till darkness fell but for pure chance. My partner lying motionless in the baking sun suddenly became an object of interest to a tiny field mouse. How this curious daredevil got past his tightly fastened belt into Ivan's tunic I still cannot understand.

While the mouse was crawling around somewhere on his back, Ivan managed to put up with it, being afraid to move. But when it ventured lower down, onto his stomach and began to nip him, Dobrik's patience snapped – he suddenly bellowed across the whole of no man's land and began laughing hysterically. I was seriously afraid. Not knowing what was happening, I thought Ivan had had a stroke from exhaustion or the scorching sun's rays. But in the meantime Ivan had discarded his rifle and was rolling around on the grass and yelling with a heart-rending voice.

'What's up, Ivan, are you out of your mind? There are Germans right next to us. They'll spray us any minute now,' I said in bewilderment

'It's a mouse! It's crawling across my belly!' was all that Dobrik could reply.

The whole situation and the expression on Ivan's face as he continued to roll around in the grass put me in a foolishly merry mood. I too began to laugh.

Of course, the Nazis were not slow to open fire with mortars.

'Let's run for it!' Ivan could barely utter the words through tears of laughter and, grabbing his rifle, he darted towards our trenches, pressing one hand to a wound he had only just suffered as he went – fragments from a mortar bomb exploding beside us had embedded themselves in his backside. I dashed after him.

We both ran upright, paying no attention to the shrapnel. It was of no significance; some kind of nervous tic contracted our cheeks – we did not even laugh, but squealed and went into spasms every time we as much as looked at each other. So, laughing all the way, we finally fell into our trenches.

'You've put on quite a show,' said the observer escorting Ivan and me under cover. 'Have you turned into a couple of half-wits, or what?' How a bullet or a significant shell fragment failed to hit us, how we avoided treading on our own mines, God only knows.

With the onset of spring our medics became concerned about infections. There were ample reasons for this. Constant mal-nourishment led to weakening of the men's constitution. Moreover, the troops were drinking untreated swampy water from shell holes because there were no other sources at hand, and the snow had already melted. True, for the meantime everything was fine thanks to the bustling activities of our battalion medical assistant, Ivan Vasilyev, who was a bright young lad. After graduating from Tambov medical school and working for a year in a rural hospital before being called up into the army, Vasilyev knew his business well. Besides that, he was a brave lad. In battle our Mikhailovich (the patronymic by which everyone addressed him), concerned himself not just with what was in front of him – patching up and evacuating the wounded – but also found time to fire back expertly at the enemy when things got tough. And one day he somehow managed to take a big strapping Nazi prisoner. Mikhailovich was constantly venturing into the heat of the action and saved the lives of hundreds of wounded men.

During lulls in the action Vasilyev was concerned with pre-ventative measures. For instance, he organised the collection of conifer needles, boiled a brew from them and got the whole battalion to drink it. This was a saviour from scurvy. He also did everything possible – and impossible – to reduce infections and stomach ailments to zero.

One day something went amiss with my stomach and I had to resort to Ivan for help. He told me to get to the medical section immediately. And so I was hoofing it to Avtovo, deep in our rear, where the medical base was located, 'for submission of all specimens and confinement in an isolation ward'. Along the way I was overtaken by a horse-drawn ambulance. The driver was a fellow-townsman of mine who had been relegated to transport duties following a serious wound. He was carting three wounded soldiers.

'Where are you heading, sniper? Hop in, I'll give you a lift!' I got up next to him on the hard seat.

The rumour that Nikolaev had been seen among the wounded found its way, with what seemed like great exaggeration, to the battalion front line. At any rate news of my funeral spread from some zealous scribe to my mother in Tambov. Twice, during the war, she received such sorrowful tidings about me . . .

After a spell in the medical centre I returned to the regiment within the allotted time. Healthy and in a good mood, I wandered round the communication routes. All around was the usual picture. All clear, all familiar, everything in its place. The fact that there were more shell holes and fewer trees in the nearby grove was nothing special. And then suddenly I heard music – somewhere the waltz 'The Torrents of the Amur' was playing loudly on the radio. This was followed by Klavdia Shulzhenko singing her renowned number 'The Blue Headscarf'. The sounds spread over the whole front line. 'Odd!' I thought.

And suddenly an announcer with a revoltingly screeching voice said: '*Achtung, Achtung*! Attention! This is German radio. Soldiers and officers of the 14th Regiment of NKVD forces, listen! Your sniper Nikolaev has been killed by our gallant soldiers. We are now also going to play 'Parting'!'

'Would you believe it! Just you wait, bloody Fritzes . . .'

I did not just walk into the command post, but stormed in. Sitting there were all the platoon commanders and the company sergeant-major. When they saw me, they glanced at one another in surprise.'

'Wow! A living corpse!,' said the sergeant-major. 'And I'd already taken you off the rations list . . .'

'We were told that they'd got you on the way to the medical centre!' said Kuzmin, the company registrar. So it was a false rumour? But there was no time to check; we've been battling with Nazis these last few days. And now the Germans have confused us . . .'

'They won't confuse us any longer!' I promised. 'Just you wait, you Nazi fibbers, I'll shove your lies down your throats! Comrade Captain, shall we show them a real funeral?' I turned to the company political adviser, Captain Zhukov.

'Why not? Let's go, Nikolaev! We'll go correct our mistake. Cover us, just in case,' the captain asked the company commander.

Armed with snipers' rifles, the political adviser and I went out onto the front line. I grabbed my cartridge pouch, which always contained a selection of different cartridges. Medical Assistant Ivan Vasilyev also asked to go with us. He equipped himself with some binoculars, which he requested from the company commander, and grabbed a submachine gun from the telephone operator.

It turned out to be a beautiful day. And even without this event I would have enjoyed the blue sky. The sun was shining high overhead, brightly illuminating everything around. The birds were twittering. Not a leaf on a tree was stirring. Peace and quiet reigned.

Choosing convenient firing positions in a gully about ten metres from our front line, we lay down and began to observe the Nazis. They were freely walking about their trenches almost without camouflage – on our sector they had not been particularly troubled over the last few days. Now the Nazis were as visible as if there were right in front of us – you could just pick one!

Lying five metres from each other, the political adviser and I did not spend long admiring the peaceful landscape. Our shots resounded and the Germans began to fall one after another. Vasilyev with the binoculars was directing us to the targets.

Eventually the political advisor called it a day: 'Well, seven between the two of us – is that enough for today? Let's not tempt fate any further.'

'Not a bad result,' Ivan Vasilyev confirmed. 'But the Germans'll start firing mortars now. Let's go. I've got no desire to drag you back wounded . . .'

When he got back to our trenches, I remembered something. 'Say, Ivan, lend me your binoculars for half an hour. Or maybe we'll go together. I want to see where the Germans have hung the radio speaker.'

'Only don't be too long, lads! The speaker's over there – it must be about eighty metres away.' And the political adviser pointed to the wood.

Ivan Vasilyev and I crawled on our elbows in the direction indicated, to where the music was coming from. Clambering into a deep shell hole, we began to look, Ivan through the binoculars and me through the telescopic sights of my rifle.

On one of the trees Ivan spotted the speaker. 'There it is! Look, there's a blue cord leading to it.'

By now I too had sighted the black bell-shape of the outdoor speaker. To aim at the cord and hit it, even from a range of a few tens of metres, would not be easy. But I remembered how we practised in our early days, attaching a matchbox to a thin twig or straw. There was no twig now, but the bright blue radio cord was clearly visible against the green background.

After lying there for a bit and completely relaxing after the rapid walk and the crawling, I got ready to fire.

'Okay, Ivan, keep looking through your binoculars. Let's see how it goes!'

After the fifth shot the music stopped. Ivan, who had kept his eye on the speaker, whispered: 'The cord has snapped as if it was cut with a knife! Now have a go at the speaker, with armour-piercing bullets! To make sure!'

I fired a few AP tracer bullets at the speaker.

'Well? What can you see?' I asked.

'I saw the bullets hit the middle of the speaker. Now I can't see anything. The speaker's still hanging there.'

'But what use is it? A bullet won't bring it down. But now it'll be silent for a long time – I know that for a fact. And that's the main thing. And now let's skedaddle out of here; the Germans will have spotted me from the tracer bullets.' We returned happily to the regiment. The German radio was silent.

But the following day, first thing in the morning the Nazis began broadcasting again, having apparently installed a new speaker overnight. With no musical introduction they announced in dreadful Russian:

> Sniper Nikolaev! Zer Fuhrer admires zer brave Russian zoldier. Our command invites you to come over to our site! It guarantees you a ferry comfortable life. You vill rezeive a big filla, haff ferry much money, Tsuker und Brot, get wedding to a Cherman Frau. Zer Fuhrer vill revard you vit a high officer's order – Iron Cross, erste class. Come ofer to our site!

What were they thinking of? What were they hoping for?

The Germans repeated their message word for word several times at intervals of ten to fifteen minutes. A few minutes later I asked permission to enter the dugout of the battalion commander, Major Morozov. Sitting in the dugout apart from him were Lieutenant Colonel Agazhin, my company commander, and Captain Zhukov.

'Well, Nikolaev,' said the battalion commander, 'did you get the invitation? Maybe you'd like to respond?'

'What have you come about, Yevgeni?' asked Lieutenant Colonel Agashin. 'I can see you've got something in mind.'

'Comrade Lieutenant Coloncl, I think Major Morozov is right; we should go and visit the Germans if they are inviting us!'

And I outlined my plan to the officers.

'Well, it's risky, even a gamble to some extent, but in principle it could work. Let's consult with our "senior" – what does he say?'

The 'senior' was 'in favour'. 'When it comes to wiping out Nazis, any means are fine!' he told Agashin.

At exactly 1900 hours I crept out of my trench and, hiding behind some bushes, crawled on my elbows in the Germans' direction, taking cover now and then in shell holes. It was still about a hundred metres to their front line. About forty metres from our trenches I arose from a shell hole and, whistling loudly, raised a white handkerchief on a stick. The Germans noticed this manoeuvre – this was apparent immediately; the firing from their side ceased. And, to the contrary, intensified from our side. But I noticed what was the main point: the Germans had begun to flock into their trenches and their heads peeped out more and more frequently along the whole line. 'Let them gather!' I was in no hurry to continue on my way.

After waiting for about ten minutes I raised myself up. 'Well, come what may! Might get away with it!' I thought and stood up to my full height. At once our 'precision' fire opened up. Single tracer bullets marked their lethal course. I again lay down in the shell hole. Then I crawled about another five metres. There were even more Germans in the trenches. I could already hear them calling: 'Komm, Komm, Soldat! Schnell, Kvickly!' I waited, as if I was afraid of them firing, even began to groan softly, as if I were wounded. There were even more Germans in the trenches. They even started shooting at our side, cutting me off, as it were, from my own forces, clearly implying that they would not touch me.

To be honest, I was quaking in my boots. What if one of our lads misses and hits me accidentally? At this point I stood up to my full height and, raising high my white handkerchief, waved it in the air, and then vigorously lowered it, thereby giving a signal . . . Not to the Germans, but to our own forces. And our mortar bombs began to whine, exploding in the German trenches. Our machine guns started up and our snipers opened fire at any

Nazi helmets that were sticking up. The bursting battalion and regimental mortars caused confusion in the German trenches and threw up an impenetrable screen of earth and dust. The dreadful howls of wounded Nazis could be heard. Under cover of this screen I made it back at the double to our own forces. Within a minute or two I was already being hugged by my friends. A prisoner, soon captured by our scouts, confirmed under interrogation that the operation had been calculated correctly; on that memorable evening the Germans lost several dozen men. We did not receive any further invitations from the Germans.

# 14.

# Our Zhenya

We had a young girl in our battalion – a medical orderly named Zhenya. Her surname I cannot recall, after so many years. All the men called her 'Our Zhenya' and that is how she has gone down in my memory.

I can see her as if she were here today, in her big *kirza* boots, her riding breeches of vast dimensions, her huge overcoat which was far too big for her, and her forage cap, which kept slipping off her shaggy head of hair. Zhenya back then was no more than sixteen years old. How and whence she had ended up in the battalion, nobody knew for certain. There were a lot of Young Communist League girls at the front, who had arrived as volunteers to defend their home city of Leningrad. She had turned up and that was all there was to it.

In order to appear older than her sixteen years, Zhenya strove to carry on like a seasoned soldier: she smoked shag tobacco, having learned how to 'roll her own', talked in a rough bass tone, and was not particular about the expressions she used . . .

While there was peace and quiet all around, nobody paid any special attention to Zhenya – just an ordinary girl, a bit cheeky, but so be it. However, they knew that in battle, whatever the situation, our Zhenya would be there where she was expected, wherever she was needed most. Therefore, they excused her whims. There was no time to deal with her re-education and nobody to do it; the Germans were only three kilometres from Leningrad and 40–100 metres from our trenches. From time to time accurate grenade-throwers would toss their missiles back and forth between the trenches.

Zhenya always had plenty of work. She saved the lives of dozens of troops, carrying seriously wounded soldiers and officers from the battlefield regardless of the rifle and machine-gun fire, the exploding shells and mines. She would patch up the lightly wounded and evacuate them to the rear, and again dash into the front line, into the very heart of the fighting. It was regarded as her normal work, like that of the soldiers themselves, or anybody else at the front, where everybody knows their job and place and takes responsibility for them.

But there was one incident involving our Zhenya which I will remember for the rest of my life.

The battalion was stationed by a mill not far from the 'Klinovo houses' near Uritsk, which were made famous by another episode in the war. It was an ordinary day at the front, the sort on which the Soviet Information Bureau would record: 'On the remaining fronts there was no significant activity.'

It was late at night before our divisional scout group ventured into the enemy's rear areas. Leading it was scout platoon commander Junior Lieutenant Ivan Pilipchuk. An excellent trainer, an intrepid scout, as well as a wag and a joker, he was everybody's favourite.

The days went by and in the trenches we waited for the return of our 'trekkers'. They ought to have been back already; it was almost two nights since they had gone. People had gathered in the trenches, ready at any moment to dash out to rescue their comrades, but everything remained as silent as before. Day had almost dawned when all those concerned by the group's long absence suddenly caught the sound of random machine-gun fire and faint but frequent grenade explosions in the enemy lines. 'It's our lot! They've been spotted! Don't say they won't break through?' each of us thought, getting ready for a charge at the German trenches if necessary. We could imagine what was happening now on the other side; however, we found out in detail when our scouts began to return to our trenches one by one, to the feverish crackle of machine-gun fire.

'What's going on there?' Everyone returning from the other side was showered with questions.

'It's not so good! We ran right into it! The officer's seriously wounded. Two killed and some have got grazes . . .'

Several agonising minutes went by. The German trenches were already visible in the blue early morning haze, but more obvious was the flight of the tracer bullets that the Nazis were firing at us. A number of men had still not returned. They included those who had been killed and would never come back, and those who were still hanging on, covering their comrades' withdrawal.

But then we caught sight of the scout platoon commander, Ivan Pilipchuk. He was the last to withdraw. Badly wounded, Pilipchuk had still managed to crawl into no man's land. Now he was lying 10–15 metres from the German trenches, in full view of the Nazis. All the rounds of Nazi machine-gun tracer firer were directed, it seemed, at one target – the escaping Soviet officer.

The firing from our side, which was on the point of stalling, started up again; Pilipchuk had to be cut off from the enemy, the Nazis could not be allowed to take him alive, and Ivan had to be helped to crawl away and get nearer to our trenches. We saw that Pilipchuk had stopped moving. We felt that he would not be able to crawl on his own. Surely it was not all over for him? No! We could hear his groans; we could see him stretching out his arms now and then. How could we help him? We all realised that it was impossible to crawl towards him; every inch of ground was swept by fire and it was now quite light.

It would have been no trouble for the Germans to finish Pilipchuk off – he was just lying there, groaning, right in front of them. But they were waiting, they were not going to touch him. They were enjoying the sight of him and of our helpless position. The Nazis could not take the lieutenant prisoner themselves; we would not let them near him.

'Russky zoldat! Rezcue zhour offitser!' shouted the Nazis, well aware that it was the law of the Red Army not to abandon a comrade in distress. Two scouts had already paid with their lives for attempting to get through to their commander. We looked at one another: what was to be done? There was no way out. The only hope was nightfall and that was almost a whole day away.

'Everybody to their posts and maintain observation! The Nazis must not be allowed near Pilipchuk, or to raise their heads!' The battalion commander, Major Morozov made a decision. 'They won't drop mortars on their own trenches! As long as he can survive till nightfall.'

And suddenly, amidst the silence that had ensured, a girl's voice rang out: 'Comrades, are we going to let the lieutenant die, or what? Some heroes! To hell with you!' A figure in a grey military overcoat had risen up, leapt out of the trench, jumped up onto the parapet and, casting off her forage cap, headed towards the German trenches.

The Germans were taken aback. Disdaining death, a girl was walking at full height to rescue her commander.

'Oh! Good woman! Come to us as prisoner!' the Nazis shouted in bad Russian, ceasing their machine-gun fire.

Now we could hear Zhenya spraying the Nazis with the foulest language and see her purposefully continuing to get nearer to the lieutenant. She went right up to him, bent down, grasped him with her arms and lifted him onto her back. And just as calmly, as if nothing was the matter, she carried him towards our trenches. Except that she was stooping ever lower under a load that was beyond her strength to bear.

'Any minute now! Any minute now the Nazis will kill her!' We froze in expectation of an unavoidable shot. But the Germans had somehow frozen at the sight of her audacity. They could not understand what had only just happened before their eyes. They had not expected such cool-headed courage from a Russian girl. And Zhenya, barely able to put one foot in front of the other, was already almost at our trenches.

'Zhenya, get down! They'll shoot you any minute!' they shouted at her from our trenches. 'Duck into a shell hole! We'll help you!'

Just ten metres from our trenches, Zhenya carefully laid down her burden on the ground. And it was only at this point that the Nazis came to. Like men possessed they opened a hurricane of fire from their machine guns, but it was too late. Our troops managed to jump out, seize the lieutenant's now limp body and lower it into a trench. With a forceful sweep someone also got Zhenya into the trench. She could hardly move on her own . . .

Our Zhenya only came to herself when the mortar bombs with which the Germans showered us had stopped whining. 'You might offer me a smoke!' she said, and immediately several hands held out tightly packed pouches and rolled cigarettes ready to smoke. Breathing heavily from what she had been through, Zhenya greedily inhaled the shag tobacco. She sat semi-recumbent with her back against the trench wall and smiled, somehow not believing that she had survived.

But just a week later our Zhenya, embarrassed by the unaccustomed attention, was presented with the Order of the Red Banner by the divisional commander in front of the regiment's assembled officers and men. It was her first decoration – for selfless courage and saving the life of a Soviet officer.

Where is our little heroine now? Did she manage to evade the Nazi bullets? Did she live to see Victory Day? And is her feat known to people in her part of the country? That remains to be found out. However, I know one thing: the scout platoon commander, Lieutenant Pilipchuk *did* survive. After enduring several subsequent operations, Ivan continued to serve in the Tambov Region – in the military, as before.

Many years have passed since we celebrated victory over Nazi Germany. I have had the opportunity to visit many cities over this period. I have seen numerous memorials set up in honour of our fallen soldiers, airmen, tank crews, gunners and sailors. But not once have I seen a memorial erected in honour of our medical staff, who saved the lives of thousands of men from all the services.

Maybe I have not seen everything. But nowhere have I read of any such monument . . .

I mention this not only because I have just remembered about our Zhenya. I benefited hugely from the efforts of military medics during the war, and I also enjoyed a firm, constant and secure friendship with the staff of the divisional medical section. It began long before the war and continues to this day, although neither the regiment, nor the division, nor even the actual medical section is still in existence; the division and all its 'auxiliaries' were disbanded back in 1945.

Military orderlies Ivan Mikhailovich Muravyov and Ivan Mikhailovich Vasilyev had graduated from the Tambov medical school in 1939. The three of us all began our military service together in the Karelian–Finnish Soviet Socialist Republic. Both Ivans then worked in the regimental medical section. Also there were the medical orderlies Vera Yarutova, Ivan Novostroyenny and Sasha Zamashkin – our regimental poet. And the head of the section, Major Sergei Nikolaevich Polikarpov, who had graduated from a medical institute just before being called up into the army, was a doctor in the regiment. However, since he was not certificated, he wore a Red Army uniform with no special markings; he still did not have full doctor's status. People in the know talked of him as a 'surgeon on whom great hopes rested'! And so it later came to pass. But back then, in 1940, we all quickly became friends. I do not remember how, except that it was not on any medical basis, as I have never been ill during peacetime. I was also on good terms with other military medical staff – maybe because I was the hardy kind and did not weary them with ailments. At any rate, when I had the chance to relax in the rear for an hour or two, I was always a welcome visitor in our divisional medical section. I just had to turn up there and my friends would instantly hand me over to the sister on duty:

'Vera, set the bath up for Nikolaev, and give him clean linen and a spare bed – let him catch up on his sleep in conditions fit for a human being.'

But they took upon themselves the most responsible and difficult task during the blockade – that of keeping me fed and plied with sweet tea.

Usually I was in the charge of my inseparable friends, nursing sisters Tamara Smolova and Vera Tatarinkova and deputy political instructor Dashunya Kopelevich, secretary of the medical section's Young Communist League organisation. They supplied me with cigarettes put aside 'for special cases' – a rationed amount which they received along with all troops and officers. I had learned to smoke during the hungry days of the siege; they were careful above providing us with tobacco. To this day I can remember with pleasure the excellent, pre-war Belomorkanal cigarettes from the Uritsk factory in Leningrad.

After I was transferred from my division to operational work with *Smersh*, I lost touch with my friends and visited them less often. But not to the extent of completely forgetting them. Our 96th Artillery Brigade, in which I served as *Smersh* counter-espionage operative, used to support units at the front with its 152 mm guns and turn up in various sectors. The instruments of the vehicles towing our big guns would record more than a dozen kilometres a day along front-line roads in pursuit of the Nazis.

But even back then, first on the Karelian Isthmus and later while liberating the Baltic area, my friends and I often met on front-line roads. I would find time between engagements and forced marches, locate the medical section, and drop in for an hour or two.

# 15.

# Back on Reconnaissance

After becoming a sniper, I did not break my ties with my friends in reconnaissance. Even now we often had to work together. I sometimes went with them on missions, carrying my own personal weapon – in case I needed to support them with sniper fire. Occasionally, I also used to go out on reconnaissance alone or in command of a group.

On one August evening in 1942 I was summoned to the battalion command post. I sensed that something was going to happen, because they would not call me just for the sake of it; at that time I found myself in a special position, being listed as a regimental sniper, although for 'housekeeping purposes' I was part of 2nd Battalion.

I reached the command post and reported my arrival as usual. Apart from the battalion commander, the general staff dugout was occupied by his deputy for operational matters, a radio operator, medical orderly Marusia Nazarova and the commander of the regiment's reconnaissance platoon.

'The regimental command has decided to entrust you with a mission, Nikolaev. The details will be outlined by the commander of the reconnaissance platoon, Lieutenant Kirsanov. Over to you, Comrade Lieutenant!'

On returning from their last mission, our scouts discovered the headquarters of a German unit. They did not have the opportunity to go in there. Now the divisional command has an urgent need for staff documents: the Nazi operational maps, orders and correspondence. The task of getting hold of them has been entrusted to our regiment. After some thought, the command decided to offer this assignment to you; you're a veteran scout and you know the enemy defences well. It's not far to go.

And he showed me the spot, which was circled in blue pencil on the 1:100,000 scale map spread out on the table.

'Staff documents to be located and brought back as per orders!' I responded.

I knew that it would not be easy. It would be necessary to cross three German defensive trench lines carefully and, having located the HQ dugout, wait a day or even more for a suitable moment to get into it. And, having done what was necessary, to return unseen to my own unit.

After a moment's silence the battalion commander said: 'No, that's not good enough. You need to take somebody with you. Let's be honest: it's a dangerous mission. You may not come back; anything could happen.'

'Comrade Major!' I said, 'It would be easier for me to complete this mission on my own. You're not just sending me out to grab a prisoner for interrogation!

And at this point the voice of medical orderly Marusia Nazarova rang out: 'Comrade battalion commander, will you give me permission to go with Nikolaev? Will you, eh . . . ?'

'That's all I need – going out on reconnaissance with a girl!' I retorted indignantly.

They all laughed simultaneously at Marusia's request. But she stubbornly repeated:

'I'll go all the same! All right, Comrade Major?'

Everyone knew that our Marusia was a brave girl; a number of times she had carried wounded soldiers and officers on her scrawny shoulders from the very heat of battle during engagements with the Nazis. But that was her day-to-day work. And this was reconnaissance.

'Comrade Major, she'll only get in my way.'

'Very well, you can go alone. But remember: don't get into a fight with the Germans and no shooting – you must not reveal yourself! There will be nobody to support you, so you must do everything nice and quietly. Break a leg! And safe return! We shall be waiting.'

And, leaning over the map, we began plotting my proposed route over and over again. We agreed on signals in the event of unforeseen circumstances, and on the location and time for my return.

'You've got the evening to get things together and get some sleep,' said the battalion commander. 'And you must be on your way during the night, with a clear head.'

What thought could there be of sleep? Back in my own dugout I checked and oiled my weapons: a Tokarev pistol, a Nagant revolver and a small Walther pistol. I would have five hand-grenades and some others in cases, a Finnish knife and that constant scout's companion – a three-colour signalling torch. All this had to be packed so that it did not make the slightest noise along the way and every object was conveniently placed for use. I stuffed all this into my pockets, boots, pack and down my shirtfront. I rubbed the buckle of my belt and my buttons with mud; I was not to carry anything shiny – the light of flares could reflect from it. Anything superfluous was removed from my pockets.

My documents also stayed at home; my Party candidate membership card I handed over to the commissar and I also left with him my two engraved watches, letters, photos and everything else. It was with some regret that I handed over the Order of the Red Banner I'd received. That is the law of reconnaissance: when you set out on an operation, you must carry nothing that can help the enemy to establish your identity – in case you are wounded or killed.

It only remained now to rehearse everything beforehand: to carry out another check, to work out how long it would take me to use a weapon – to draw the knife, throw a grenade, fire the pistol, to grab another one, to be ready to fire, either right- or left-handed, to fire through my trouser pockets or padded jacket, and from inside my shirt-front. We organised these rehearsals ourselves – they were always useful. Even with a sniper's rifle I learned, while walking with the weapon over my shoulder, to prepare on command 'for action' with a count of one rather than the regulation three. It was a very deft and dramatic move; you seize the neck below the butt with your right hand and 'hey presto!' – the rifle spins in the air and, in an instant, you have it ready for firing.

Beyond the door of my dugout it was already night – dark, moonless and impenetrable. That was not altogether a bad thing to begin with. I was escorted on my way. There was our front line; there was our last outpost. A final farewell from the battalion commander, final instructions from the reconnaissance platoon commander, synchronisation of watches and specification of signals. A brief, friendly farewell – a pat on the shoulder or back. A last handshake with friends and a light push upwards, over the parapet of the trench. And I would merge with the landscape.

But I was still not alone; I was now accompanied by an experienced sapper who would help me to get through the barrier of mines – both our own and the enemy's, although the path through our own mine belt was already well known to me. For the moment the sapper went ahead of me. But then he extended his hand and waved with the other one: 'I'm off!'

Now I was all alone in the pitch darkness. As always at the start of a mission, I felt a little uncomfortable. Only for a few seconds, but it was a bit scary. Exactly the sort of fear experienced by everyone returning to the front-line trenches after lengthy treatment in hospital: for two to three days you duck at every bullet flying past and stoop low after every shell explodes. But then you feel at home again and pay no attention to the whistle of fragments from an exploding shell nearby. Likewise, now I just needed to adjust to the situation, get used to being on my own, remember the task I had been set – and everything would be all right. However, it was time to move on, to meet the unknown.

I passed safely across the first trench in the German defences. I had long studied it and knew it like the back of my hand. Accompanied by the rattle of machine-gun fire from both sides, but deliberately started by our own, I crossed the second line of trenches just as successfully. Pausing a moment to take a breath and have a look around, I then continued moving forward towards the final, third, trench-line. Here it was easier for me; the Germans felt they could operate more freely than on the front line, be more relaxed, talk more loudly, and go around without concealing themselves. Thus, it was easier for me to find my bearings. However, their loud speech was not merely due to feeling relaxed – they were afraid of the dark Russian night and therefore tried to cheer themselves up by talking.

Even here their flares were still flying up into the sky, albeit less frequently. They hindered rapid movement, but at the same time helped you to work out where you were. While flares were hanging in the air by their tiny parachutes, I would press myself close to the ground and freeze, while looking all around. Beside me ran a ditch leading to the staff dugout – until you got to a large clump of bushes. It would be easier to follow the ditch, but it was out of the question; it was periodically raked by German fire, just in case. I crawled parallel to the ditch. There was the stream – everything was where it should be! I was on the right track and now almost at the target. The dugout I was after should be just a little to the left of the 'free-standing tree'. I moved carefully in that direction, concealed by the thick bushes. The soft grass muffled all the rustling. Like a grass snake I crept up close to the sound of voices – there it was, the dugout itself! Pacing up and down nearby was a sentry, who was talking loudly to someone. I moved towards the sound of his voice and unexpectedly fell into some sort of pit.

'A shell hole, damn it!' I guessed. Well, it could be very handy at the moment.

Little by little I crept up towards the opposite edge and carefully raised my head – the dugout was right beside me. Now all my attention was concentrated on it: who would go in, for how long, and when they would come out?

Then four Germans came out of the dugout together and dispersed in pairs along the trench in different directions. I tried to work it out mentally, how many of them were there in total? Who was now left inside? There could be another four: an officer, his batman, a radio operator and possibly a sentry for the next shift. I lay there, almost without breathing, and listened. Were the Germans going to start talking? Maybe I could learn something from their conversation?

Once more I remembered my Tambov school with gratitude – it had trained me well! All the knowledge obtained within its walls had come in handy on the front, especially the foreign language. Huge thanks were due to our teacher, Varvara Afanasyevna Belyaeva. Under her direction we had put on whole plays in German on the school stage and I had always played the lead roles in them.

Again the dugout door opened, and out came one more Nazi. I sensed he was a tall because his bass voice was audible much higher up than the level of the trenches. And when he had moved a few metres away from the dugout, I saw indeed how high his silhouette stood. The sniper within me spoke up: 'You should fire now at the silhouette!' The thought flashed through my mind, but instantly vanished again; the Beanpole approached the sentry and began to tell him something. I listened in. So far as I could understand, the Beanpole was off to Uritsk, to the rear, for a *Frau*!

'Thinking of recreation, the bastards! Just you wait! You'll pay for this too, just give us time!' I thought.

I worked it out and decided that there could be only one or two people in the dugout now. What should I do? Was I going to be lying there waiting for a long time? Dawn could come quickly – then it would be all over for me.

All around it was silent; all I could hear was muffled footsteps in the distance – the sentry walking up and down the trench, somewhere about twenty metres from the dugout. I was a little startled and distracted by a suspicious rustle – somewhere to the right and a long way behind me. But the rustling ceased and I calmed down. Somehow it was not a threat to me – I realised this from some special scout's sense. I could not have left 'traces' of myself and the Germans were apparently relaxed.

However, my attention was partly focussed in that direction; would the rustling be repeated? No, nothing could be heard for the moment. Now I was overcome by a nervous trembling. This always happens in the face of any danger, after you have taken a decision and the time has come to act on it. To act on your own, when you are your own commanding officer and your own subordinate, and the whole operation is in your hands, as well as your own life.

But this was not from fear; no, it was not that kind of trembling! It was from a feeling of arousal before a decisive thrust, real action. I had devised a precise plan by which I would have to operate, a plan calculated down to the last second.

It seemed that not even ten minutes had passed since the Beanpole had left, but someone else came out of the dugout. He remained standing for a little, stamped his feet, listened all around, and clicked his cigarette lighter – he was having a smoke. Then he called in both directions: 'Wie heiss?' – 'How are things?', in other words. 'Alles sehr gut!' the sentry replied.

Well, I thought so too; so far everything was going very well.

I sensed that it was the occupant of the dugout who had emerged. Seemingly, he was supposed to check the sentry posts, and he was either being lazy or was afraid to go too far away. But he should have done . . . !

Well, that was it! The moment seemed to have arrived. If he doesn't go farther now and returns to the dugout, he will have to be taken out. 'As long as there's no noise,' I remembered. The Finnish knife was already in my hands, its blade concealed in the sleeve of my tunic, so that it did not gleam. I squeezed the handle powerfully and got ready to crawl into the trench.

But I was in luck. Reassured that everything nearby was 'sehr gut', the German had taken the risk of finally walking a little farther along the trench. It was after all the third line, deep in the rear. His steps began to fade slowly into the distance. He seemed calm, but I was agitated: I had no right to wait any longer! I would have to take care of the others in the dugout, if indeed there were any. It would be good if they were asleep.

I slid into the trench right by the door. Slowly I pulled it towards me. It opened without a sound and I carefully stepped into the unknown. Inside it was quiet. Dimly burning on the table was a Russian 'Lightning' kerosene lamp, with its top chipped where it met the glass. It spread a soft light around.

I had a matter of minutes to complete my task; the officer could return at any moment. Just in case I had a grenade ready for action; I could use it first as a hammer – hit the officer on the head with it. The pistol was also to hand, in case of extreme emergency. I took a quick look around. On the solidly built log wall hung a big portrait of Hitler in a glassless frame. Stuck on at all angles around the portrait were a couple of dozen postcards and photos cut out from magazines of naked beauties in various poses. 'They make appropriate neighbours!' I thought.

Around the lamp on the table stood some wine bottles, which were either empty or not yet opened. There were also some snacks on plates, open tins of food, and bread. I was looking for what was most important and, hanging over a nickel-plated double bed I saw an officer's field bag, three gas masks, and two submachine guns.

I grabbed the field bag without looking in it and hung it over my shoulder and under my belt, so it would not dangle, and I took the magazines out of the submachine guns and thrust them in the tops of my boots. The bag was still not everything. Where was the important stuff? Piled one on top of the other near the table were three wooden shell boxes. It was our practice to use them to store staff documents. I easily opened the lid of the top box, but apparently to no purpose; it contained . . . female underwear.

I crept under the bed, where there were another two such boxes, except that one of them was bound with iron. I dragged it out. It was not locked, fortunately. I opened it and saw that this was it, the stuff I had been sent for!

I had only just started to stuff the cards and documents into my pockets and down my shirt-front, when, suddenly, I caught the sound of cautiously approaching steps. My nerves and hearing were strained to the limit. I dashed over to the door and pressed myself sideways against the wall with a grenade raised high in one hand. With the other, left, hand I gripped the handle of the Finnish knife. And suddenly I heard a soft whisper from outside:

'Yevgeni, are you there? Open up! It's me, Marusia!'

I cautiously opened the door – it was her! Come to pay a visit! I dragged her into the dugout by the scruff of the neck and went numb, unable for an instant to articulate a word.

Finally, I acquired the gift of speech and said: 'So it's you, Marusia, you bitch!' and I poked the grenade and the Finnish knife under her nose. 'Have you any idea what I would like to do to you now?'

'But I want to see how reconnaissance is carried out,' Marusia replied imperturbably and looked at me pitifully.

'She's a devil woman, not a child!' I thought. 'How did she creep up like that, so I didn't hear her? Where has she been all this time?'

Then, calming down a little, I said: 'Well, take a look! What's so interesting about it? At least you haven't brought anybody after you, have you?'

'No, the officer was chatting with the sentry, and they were having a smoke! So I came in after you. I saw you. I was beside you the whole time! But I was afraid to call out . . .'

Fobbing her off with a wave of the hand, I began rifling through the boxes again. I also searched under the pillows and under the mattress. Marusia helped me, stuffing the documents in her first-aid bag.

'Time to go! It'll be harder getting out of here than getting in,' I told Marusia, bearing in mind her presence, which I had not reckoned on.

Grabbing a couple of submachine guns and casting a final glance round the dugout, I snuffed out the lamp and unscrewed the top from it. I poured the kerosene all around, splashed some on the boxes and pulled a blanket off the bed.

'Come on! You go out first and cover the entrance with the blanket! I'll be right with you!' Grabbing a couple of dinner knives from the table, I struck a match and leapt out the door.

I gave Marusia one knife and showed her what she needed to do. We fastened the blanket over the door, sticking the knives I had taken into the upper corners. They easily went into the grooves.

By the time we had left the second trench line, flames had flared up, exploding from the dugout we had only just left. There was, however, no commotion; apparently, as I had counted on, the German officer thought the fire had been started by the kerosene lamp. Thus, we were safely able to jump over the first German trench. Stopping a little while to get our breath back in a shell hole along the way, we moved on farther. On the way back I crawled ahead of Marusia, because she had most probably forgotten where the path through the minefield lay. I did not look back, but I knew that Marusia was cautiously moving behind me, copying all my movements. And I could not hear her! Not a single branch snapped under her and not a single bush quivered.

And only when we were in our own trenches did I give vent to the fury which was tearing me apart.

'Don't make a fuss, soldier!' Marusia answered me. She stood there and smiled as if nothing was the matter . . .

Subsequently the army newspapers often wrote about the feats of our medical orderly Marusia Nazarova, who carried a good few hundred wounded soldiers and officers from the field of battle during the heavy fighting near Leningrad, and noted her courage and her selfless devotion to the motherland.

# 16.

# Brave Girls

It was 1942. We had not put aside our weapons for almost a year. My sniper's rifle had become my third eye and my third hand; it helped me to search for, locate and annihilate the enemy. I gained experience in trench warfare, which I perfected with every passing day – in duels with German snipers, in the art of camouflaging myself and detecting camouflaged Nazis, and in shooting both by day and by night.

I willingly shared my experience not only with my comrades – already experienced snipers – but first and foremost with marksmen who were just starting out. I instructed many officers and men in the sniper's art during this period. My pupils also included women. It is no secret that, even back in peacetime, women were allowed to serve, albeit rarely, in the ranks of the Red Army. They became particularly numerous during the war. They held various posts – from the humble duties of typist, medical orderly in a detachment, cook, laundress and wireless operator, to those of pilots and tank crew, to say nothing of the women who were doctors, interpreters, teachers, investigators, and so on.

Everybody knew the name of the legendary partisan Zoya Kosmodemyanskaya, from the village of Vederevshchina in the Tambov region, who was posthumously awarded the lofty title of

Hero of the Soviet Union. Also widely known was the renowned Sevastopol sniper, Hero of the Soviet Union Lyudmila Pavlichenko.

Returning one day from the divisional general staff to my regiment after yet another snipers' meeting, I happened to walk past a detachment of mortar bombers. It was located in a stone factory-style building on the right-hand side of the highway to Uritsk. Suddenly I heard somebody call out:

'Hey, Comrade sniper! Just a minute!'

I stopped and looked around. Approaching me was a girl in a military uniform with a first-aid bag over her shoulder. She stretched out her hand with long, delicate fingers and said:

'Barely caught you up! Well, let's get to know each other. I am Medical Orderly Marusya Mitrofanova, lance-corporal. And I know who you are.'

We got talking. It turned out she had a request of me – to teach her sniping.

'My pleasure, Comrade Mitrofanova!'

She did not give me any details about herself on that occasion. But later I learned from lads I knew that she was a member of the Young Communist League from Leningrad. She had not been accepted for military service at the enlistment office on account of her age, but she had got her own way nevertheless – she left for the front line with the militia and managed to see some fighting. Her older brother was fighting the Nazis somewhere nearby, but in a different division. And she had a mother, three sisters and four brothers left in Leningrad. Her father had died in 1936 when Marusya was only thirteen. She was the youngest in the family.

'You don't smoke, do you?' I asked her unexpectedly.

'I indulge a little. What of it?'

'Just that you must drop it! If you're going to smoke, I won't take you. What if you start coughing in an ambush? Then we've both had it.'

'I'll give it up!'

Marusya turned out to be a bright pupil. Within a few days she was already accurately hitting home-made targets, grouping the bullets tightly round the bull's eye. And the first time she went out 'hunting', she wiped out two Nazis at once.

Marusya became particularly bad-tempered after she had been wounded for the umpteenth time by a fragment of a shell that exploded nearby. This time she was hit in the mouth – her lower lip. She did not go to hospital, but spent time in the divisional medical section. She was given the chance to travel to Moscow, which had a special cosmetic surgery institute where she could have an excellent operation done on her, but she flatly refused.

'I haven't got time now to mess around in the rear!'

They sewed her lip up in our medical section. And Marusya looked none the worse for it. Except that her face began to look even bolder.

In the lulls between battles Marusya Mitrofanova would come looking for me in the regiment and we would set off hunting for Nazis.

'Be economical with your cartridges,' I taught her. 'Keep cool and only fire when you're certain. If you feel you won't hit the target, don't fire, or else you may not get to take another shot. There are lots of Germans and plenty of choice. But don't hurry; that doesn't always help. Don't just aim at soldiers, but go for the higher ranks – that's our main objective.'

Marusya wiped out sixteen Nazis with me and, after three weeks, she was going out 'hunting' on her own. She was not afraid of the difficulties involved, but did not rush in without thinking, did not take risks for nothing – she knew the cost of a sniper's bullet.

I correspond to this day with Marusya, who has for a long time not been Mitrofanova but Barskova. She lives in Leningrad and carries out major community work for patriotic and military purposes. At the moment she is the executive secretary of our divisional veterans' committee. She has also brought up two daughters who are just like their mother.

\* \* \*

Regimental commissar Ivan Ilyich Agashin promised to recommend me for Party membership. He called me in for a chat at the regiment command post at 1500 hours one day.

The sentry guarding the commissar's dugout said: 'Wait a bit, Nikolaev, the commissar's busy at the moment. He'll call you in himself. Sit down for a little, relax.'

Taking off my waterproof cape, I folded it and perched on a stump under the green canopy of a tree that stood about ten metres from the commissar's dugout.

Around twenty minutes went by. The rain which had overtaken me on the way had stopped and the sun peeped out. The regimental postman handed me some letters for the battalion. There was one there for me from Tambov.

I opened the envelope. At home everything was in order and, as always, Mum was waiting for her son to come home after victory. Immediately my heart felt warmer.

Suddenly a girl with a forage cap in her hands came out of the dugout. 'Possibly a new typist or an orderly from the medical section – who knows?' I thought. You could not see the tabs under her raincoat.

'Why no greeting?' she asked suddenly.

I jumped up, put on my own cap, stretched myself up to my full height and raised one hand to my temple.

'Let's get to know each other. I'm Margarita Borisovnna Kotikovskaya, military investigator for the divisional prosecution office.' And she was the first to extend her hand.

I guessed that she had not just spoken to me without good reason. And I was a little concerned; why would I have been of interest to the divisional prosecution office?

'Teach me to shoot with a sniper's rifle!'

I was astounded. This was unexpected.

'Don't you believe me? Take a look!'

And she pointed to a telegraph pole. On it some curling, torn-off wires were swaying in the wind, while some lonely green 'cups' showed up on the metal cross-pieces. Three shots rang out, one after the other, and, after each one, green fragments splashed onto the ground.

'There you are!' said Margarita Borisovna, putting her Tokarev pistol away in its holster.

'Impressive!' I said. 'Neatly done.'

I was convinced that Margarita Borisovna was a crack shot. But that is not enough to be a Nazi killer. Anyone can fire at a target. True, not everyone will hit it, but let's assume they do. However, the real skill lies in finding the target, tracking it down.

I decided to teach Margarita Borisovna this skill. She arrived at our front line two weeks after that memorable encounter at the regimental command post. I took a spare sniper's rifle and we set off for the front line. At first Margarita Borisovna only came along as a partner, observed my operations and got herself acclimatised to the environment. I specially chose the safest firing sites for her, which she of course did not suspect. At the same time, I taught my diligent pupil what a sniper needs to know and to be able to do: how to operate in different environments, and how to act in any situation. She grasped everything instantly and proved quick on the uptake.

However, she quickly realised that I was just spoon-feeding her. Then I decided that her period of probation was over and it was time for my pupil to move on to practical operations. This appealing and courageous girl wiped out thirty Nazis in my presence alone. She now lives and works in Leningrad.

# 17.

# Guests of the Kirov Workers

On 1 May 1942, Ivan Dobrik and I were summoned to divisional headquarters. Back in the regiment we had been told: 'Report to Matveyev, head of the divisional political department.'

Ivan and I had long been acquainted with Regimental Commissar Matveyev, a short, lean man with the upright bearing of a veteran regular military officer, handsome features and a stern and intelligent look. In the regiment we saw Matveyev often, and every one of our troops and officers respected and liked him. He was demanding, but always fair. He was unpretentious in his behaviour, fond of the troops and they repaid him in kind.

'You are going as divisional representatives to the Kirov works, which sponsor us; you've been invited to a formal gathering for May Day,' said Matveyev after greeting us. 'You are required to be there at 1400 hours. It's possible that you'll have to say a few words. Get going now, or you'll be late. Don't hang around there too long – it's not an appropriate time for that . . . And report as soon as you get back. Here is your authorisation. Nikolaev is in charge.'

We had two hours to walk the four kilometres separating the divisional command post from the Kirov works. The route was, to put it frankly, not the easiest; the Nazis were shelling the highway and everything around it.

Not a single vehicle overtook us on the way. Very occasionally we encountered a lone traveller heading towards the front – either communications officers or people like us on special missions. More often than not we overtook wounded troops and officers heading for the rear, those who had made it to first aid posts with the help of medical orderlies.

The closer we got to the city, the more we encountered control points, at which we were required each time to show our authorisation along with our Red Army identification. The control points were manned by troops and officers in peaked caps with a green band – from the NKVD border guards. They thoroughly checked our documents and, having done so, wished us a pleasant journey, warning us about the most dangerous places along the road.

Within about 500 metres of the famous Kirov works Ivan and I stopped to tidy ourselves up; removing our tunics, we shook the grime of the trenches out of them. We immediately sewed on fresh collars – made from pieces of cheesecloth folded in four, as I had already used up the individual allowance from my secret supplies. With the aid of some sand and soil and a bit of saliva we painstakingly polished our buckles and buttons. In the absence of a shoe brush we wiped the dust off our *kirza* boots with grass. And only then, after giving each other a critical look, did we decide that we looked fairly respectable.

It was with some agitation that we approached the passage through which Kirov and Kalinin had entered the works, and where the great Lenin had passed a number of times. We arrived a little before the set time, and so, stopping on the opposite side of the street, we cooled down after our rapid walk, while awaiting our escort; he had still not appeared.

A wizened old woman went past us, barely able to put one foot in front of the other. Despite the warmth of the day she was covered by a woollen scarf tied cross-ways across her back. Her eyes were sad and her face wrinkled and grey. Suddenly she stopped, and, taking a close look at us, asked: 'What are those pretty decorations of yours for, sons?'

'We're snipers. We knock out Nazis, granny,' I answered.

'And have you wiped out many of them?'

'We would like it to be more. He's accounted for 152 and I've got 124.'

On hearing this, the old dear wailed almost at a chant: 'Thank you to you, my lovely boys! If only every soldier was like that! Then my Victor would still be alive . . .'

'We'll avenge your Victor, absolutely, granny!'

'And you must have mothers waiting for you at home?' she asked.

'Too true – they're waiting for us, of course! But excuse us, we're running late.'

'Well, a pleasant journey and good luck!' And, waving us good-bye, she went on her way. We slung our snipers' rifles onto our backs and hurried to the entrance.

The room our escort led us into was crowded. Knowing that the works were continuously shelled by the enemy, I asked: 'Isn't it dangerous for you to have so many people gathered in one place?' I received the calm reply: 'A little bit! But we're used to it – like you, we've learned not to be afraid of shelling. We've got shelters and we've dug burrows, but the Kirov staff don't always use them – the work can't wait! If we sat it out in bomb shelters, who would make the shells and repair the tanks?'

We were seated at the presidium table, which was covered by a calico cloth. We looked around. Sitting before us were the delegates from the factory's workshops, who had come straight from their lathes clad in their greasy padded jackets, gas-masks over their shoulders and rifles in their hands. Thin, grey and emaciated, their faces remained stern even on this festive day.

The meeting commenced as soon as Ivan and I sat down. As if they were just waiting for us.

Comrades! Today's formal gathering dedicated to the
First of May is being attended by two esteemed guests
– the top soldiers of the NKVD 21st Rifle Division,
which is sponsored by our works – outstanding snipers
from the Leningrad Front, Deputy Political Instructor
Yevgeni Nikolaev and Ivan Dobrik. Each of them has
wiped out over a hundred Nazis. How they achieved
this, they will tell us themselves. But in the meantime
let us welcome these dear defenders of our land.

All those gathered in the hall stood up together and began to
applaud.

'Allow me to read the text of a telegram sent by the commander
of this division, Colonel Panchenko, in which, on behalf of the high
command and its personnel, he greets us all on this occasion,' said
the chairman and, to thunderous applause, read out the telegram
which I had previously handed over to the presidium. The formal
gathering proceeded in a business-like fashion. In front-line style,
it was brief and to the point.

Ivan and I did not know the names of the people sitting beside
us. One of them, apparently the works Party organiser, gave not so
much a May Day speech as a condensed report on the achievements
with which the Kirov staff were greeting this occasion. Referring
to the working difficulties created by wartime conditions, he said
that the works collective had coped with the objective it had been
set and would cope with any commission in the future as well.

The works were right next to the front line. Dozens of bombs
and shells destroyed workshops and equipment every day and put
people out of action. The lack of the essential specialists, most of
whom had been moved to the Urals, the acute shortage of fuel and
raw materials, the hunger, and the cold had not broken the will
of the workers remaining in Leningrad. They were confident of
victory.

In workshops wrecked by enemy shells, tanks, howitzers and
guns were being repaired and shells were being manufactured for

the front. On occasion crews composed of the factory's workers would man the repaired tanks and set off directly for the front line and straight into battle with the Nazis. Specially organised repair teams would set off for the front line and carry out repairs to tanks and ordnance on the spot during battle. And, if necessary, members of the team would load and carry the shells, or even drive the tanks. Many Kirov staff had joined the militia and had long been fighting at the front. The women and children took their places at the lathes, replacing the husbands and fathers who had gone to the front. Addressing those gathered, the speaker called for maximum efforts to bring about a complete rout of the Nazis.

The speech was followed by the presentation of awards to leaders in productivity. A directive read out from the works director noted veterans of labour and the factory's top workers. As one who had attended many similar ceremonial occasions before the war, I was surprised that neither on the presidium table nor in its vicinity were there any of the items customary in such cases – gramophones, guitars, pieces of cloth, cameras and other gifts, which were generally prepared beforehand for presentation. Ivan had similar thoughts.

'What are they going to reward them with? Where are the prizes?' he whispered.

'We'll find out right now.'

'For excellent results in his work, for training young qualified staff, for personal courage, and for fulfilment of a special order ahead of schedule, our renowned decorated master, Bushtyrkov, Sergei Mikhailovich, is awarded . . .'

And how surprised Ivan and I were when, to a storm of applause from those sitting in the hall, the distinguished master went up to the table and was presented with two chits for supplies from the factory stores . . . half a kilo of olive oil and a kilogram of joiner's glue. In response to my bewildered look, a neighbour at the table said:

'Don't be surprised! For us at the moment it's the most precious prize. With the bucket of carpenter's glue, you can make a bucketful of jelly – enough to feed a family for several days. And with the olive oil you can fry something.'

Well, this man was right to be pleased for the master and his award. The food situation in the city was still very difficult. Although there had been several additions to the bread ration and those employed in busy workshops already received by then 700 grams per day, ordinary works 500 grams, salaried staff 400 grams, and children and dependents 300 grams, it was very little for people emaciated by hunger.

When the prizes, certificates and other awards had been presented and the recipients had left, I was given the floor. I had not prepared specially for this occasion and did not know what I would say to the workers. However, my impressions of the day, everything I had seen and heard at the factory, came to my assistance. The words came of their own accord.

After thanking them for their invitation and congratulating the collective on the occasion of May Day, I voiced the wish that they would all live to see Victory Day. I conveyed thanks as a soldier for their active assistance for the front as a whole and to us, troops of the 21st Division in particular, and for the courageous political instructor of our company, Vladimir Mikhailovich Lapko, who had been trained at the Kirov works. I described how we and they were fighting together and how bravely the other Kirov staff were battling – such as political instructor Ulyanov, my sniping pupil Private Vinogradov, battalion commander Morozov, and many others. I also had to talk about the way Ivan and I were wiping out Nazis and to recall several battle episodes.

I was given an attentive hearing and questions followed. My agitation proved unwarranted. Everything seemed to go off well.

'I can't talk better than my friend and partner, Yevgeni! I'm better at shooting Fritzes; I'm no good with words. I promise to wipe out 300 Nazis and even more if I'm still alive,' said Ivan Dobrik, mixing Russian words with Ukrainian in his agitation.

He got, if anything, warmer applause than I did – for a brief and pithy speech.

Returning to the regiment, Ivan Dobrik and I told the troops what we had seen and heard at the Kirov works. Our comrades listened to us without interrupting. Shaken by what they had heard, they swore to destroy even more Nazis. They promised to exact vengeance on the hated invaders on behalf of the mutilated city of Leningrad, its brave residents, children and old men, and its heroic working class. Our snipers pledged themselves to improving their battle expertise, to multiply their ranks on a daily basis by training others in the sniper's art, and to increase their own personal score in the extermination of the Nazi scum.

# 18.

# From the Soviet Information Bureau . . .

It was the second half of June 1942. Suddenly one day, quite unexpectedly, an unaccustomed silence descended on our regiment's sector. For over two days now this silence had delighted us and, at the same time, put us on our guard. It seemed to be putting pressure on our eardrums, which, right from the beginning of the war, had managed to get used to sounds that never ceased for a minute: the crashing of bombs and shells, the whine of mortars and the rattle of exploding grenades, the hurried babble of machine guns, the whistle of bullets pursuing one another, the loud, clear curt commands of the officers, the cries of 'Hurrah!' and the groans of wounded comrades.

And now, in this unexpected silence, we discovered that we had not forgotten, it seemed, how to talk quietly, to hear one another distinctly. We even had some free time in which we could write long letters home or simply sit and do nothing. In wearisome expectation of something, we gazed at the boundless blue sky till our eyes got sore and discovered that it was the same as it had been before the war. We also noticed that the days were long, sunny and hot, and the nights short and also hot. The grass, it turned out, was still growing and waving, and you could still relax by lying down on it, looking up at the sky. And quite close by, just beyond the parapets of the trenches, bluebells and daisies were growing and stretching up towards the sun on their slender stems. We saw bumblebees flying past, and heard their buzzing distinctly. Even the flutter of dragonfly wings flitting above us was audible. Only the occasional isolated rifle shots of snipers in the enemy's direction and blinding flares hissing up at night – that was all that broke the silence that had descended.

'There's something funny about all this,' the battalion commander, Senior Lieutenant Arkhipov, told Lieutenant Popov of our company, who was reporting on the situation in our sector of the front line. 'It's even ringing in my ears! Don't relax, Lieutenant, be ready for anything unexpected. And in the meantime let your troops carry on deepening the trenches and dig more foxholes. And observation! Don't drop your guard for a minute. I've got a feeling the Nazis are up to something!'

And we observed. Every metre in the enemy defences was scrutinised more thoroughly than before. The slightest change there and in the landscape before us, with which we were familiar down to the smallest details, was picked up and recorded in reports.

And during the daylight hours of 21 July Lieutenant Popov was already reporting to battalion commander Arkhipov by telephone: 'My observation team have reported major enemy troop movement from the rear up to our front line!'

The same day there was another call to the battalion commander after nightfall. 'I can hear the noise of engines in the distance. Sounds like tanks. How many there are there I can't establish without reconnaissance. It's quiet here in the meantime, very quiet, you could say!' the company commander stressed.

'Strengthen the observation posts and put the company on full battle readiness. Stock up on ammunition, have some petrol bombs urgently delivered, and take some more anti-tank grenades. Station the anti-tank gunners more rationally. And I'll report your thoughts about the enemy – the 1st Battalion was interested in your sector in particular. They're waiting for reports.'

The troops stood tensely at their posts; observers tracked the enemy defences more closely than before. They listened to what was happening now beyond the railway embankment, which ran along no man's land, dividing the gully between our trenches in two. Apparently the Nazis were gathering there for a decisive assault; curt, barking commands resounded and the noise of engines and clang of weapons could be heard.

All became clear the following day, 22 July 1942. It was here, in our battalion's sector, that the Nazis decided to break through to Leningrad whatever the cost. At exactly 1000 hours their air force thoroughly bombed our entire defences and then their artillery and mortar bombers 'worked over' the front line for around thirty minutes. The din was unbelievable and for some time everything around went dark. Earth flew up in the air. In a few minutes what had been a flat, green and peaceful gully was transformed beyond recognition – everything around was smoking, with a revolting stench of sulphur.

Standing in the close confines of a rifleman's lair with my sniper's weapon in my hands, I distinctly heard the earth in the trenches cave in from the explosion of shells. During the first minutes of artillery fire our trenches were damaged in many places and some of our dugouts were destroyed.

It was a tough day for the troops, who were stationed 10–15 metres from one another. Some were killed or wounded. Our already diminished ranks thinned noticeably after this bombardment – in my company there were only twenty-three men, including officers, to defend a 500-metre line . . .

Those who remained alive hurriedly prepared to repel the enemy attack, which was to be expected any minute. The troops dug their comrades out, and recovered weapons and ammunition. Where possible they fixed them up and repaired the wrecked firing positions, dugouts and the collapsed trenches. Medical orderlies offered first aid to the wounded and then dealt with the dead.

Officers clarified losses and gave orders. Observers who had sat in their foxholes during the bombardment instantly moved into firing positions, feeling for the petrol bombs and fused grenades, which had been placed conveniently to hand. The machine gunners and anti-tank crews cleaned the earth and sand off their weapons, placed them on the parapets for convenience, and hurriedly cleared and improved the firing sector in front of them. Nobody remained with nothing to do, but there was no unnecessary fuss either. Everyone knew what he would do if a burst of machine-gun fire from attacking Nazis descended on our trenches. We were ready to meet them.

And they came . . . The artillery had barely fallen silent before dense lines of Nazis began to appear from behind the railway embankment and crawl along the gully. Launched against us was a band of strapping, well-fed, frenzied Germans, urged on by their officers. The soldier next to me in the trench placed his helmet more firmly on his head and, to nobody in particular, announced:

'It's started . . . Well, brothers, we won't break this time either!' And he critically inspected the grenades and petrol bombs laid out in front of him.

Someone heard him and immediately called back: 'It's not the first time we've beaten the bastards, and we'll do it again now – just let them stick their heads up!'

Pressing their machine guns into their stomachs, the Germans kept coming, spraying the trenches with unaimed fire. We were being charged by a horde up to two battalions in strength. Our trenches remained silent. We had seen such frenzied attacks before, so we were not frightened by this one. Neither were we intimidated by the fact that a couple of dozen troops were facing an avalanche of Germans in their frog-green uniforms. Nor did we fear the rattle of their machine guns – we knew that such unaimed fire only affects the psyche and is intended for those with weak nerves, and there were none like that among us. We decided to let this drunken mob closer to us in order to be certain of hitting it, so we could fire selectively. As soon as the Nazis had completely

174

swarmed across the railway embankment, filled the gully, and begun to approach within twenty or thirty metres of our trenches, our machine gunners were the first to open fire.

Anatoly Shcherbinsky mowed down a good few dozen Nazi bandits with his Maxim gun and machine gunner Nikolai Guly was not far behind. Behind them the riflemen of the company fired in a coordinated and calculated fashion. With my sniper's rifle I shot at officers and those soldiers who were almost right up to our trenches. The barrel of my rifle grew red-hot . . .

Not expecting to encounter such fierce resistance, the Nazis began a hurried retreat. Some of the German survivors took cover in shell holes and started hastily digging in. The others, left without their officers, faltered, and ran back, leaving dozens of bodies in the gully. But at this point artillery and mortars came into play from the depths of our defences. What the riflemen had started was finished off by their friends, the gunners. The first attempt of the Nazi cut-throats to break through our defences choked.

We got a lot of help from an anti-aircraft battery attached to the regiment and stationed somewhere in the depths of its defences. These gunners used their fire to cut the enemy off from the railway embankment, prevented them from getting away, and finished them off on the spot, in the gully. Few of them succeeded in escaping righteous vengeance on this occasion.

Commanding the anti-aircraft battery was Senior Lieutenant Yushin, another Tambovian, whom I had recently met by chance – the same Semyon Yushin who had attended school with me back home. Reckless even in his schooldays, he now took the decision, in spite of the danger, to move his battery forward to deliver direct fire and coolly swept the Nazis with anti-aircraft machine-gun fire and bombarded them with high explosive shells, annihilating the enemy's mortar crews. And Yushin's intrepid AA gunners fired just as accurately at ground as at aerial targets. Now, in addition to bringing down several aeroplanes, the battery knocked out the enemy mortars. The role of 'spotter' on this occasion was fulfilled by the battery's deputy commander for political instruction, Senior

Political Instructor Dmitry Martynovich Yerofeyev, who was in our trenches during this battle. Again and again he telephoned his battalion commander that the Germans were gathering beyond the embankment for a new assault. But the battery commander himself could already see through his binoculars what was happening in our sector. All it took was a brief order, and the fire of the anti-aircraft guns again descended on the Nazis. Once again the company machine gunners would not let the Nazis raise their heads; again I put their officers and their more zealous soldiers out of action.

With the aid of the AA gunners the second attempt by the enemy infantry to attack our trenches also fizzled out. And yet the situation remained critical; we did not have enough troops, almost all the officers had been disabled, and the enemy were capable of repeating their attacks. Of the two Nazi battalions a good half were now left lying eternally in this gully. But what if this assault was only for reconnaissance? To test their forces and ours? What if they suddenly throw a whole regiment at us? In such a case we could not hold our ground, even with artillery support. But no soldier even conceived of abandoning his position and handing trenches over to the enemy. That would mean letting the Nazis through to Leningrad! Left as we were, devoid of communication with the regiment, we were not sure that the commanders were aware of our developing situation and already taking measures to render assistance to the thin ranks of the garrison. In fact, the assistance arrived almost in good time. But while we waited we again tidied up our trenches and got ready to repel fresh enemy attacks, which were not slow in being renewed.

Within half an hour or so the replenished Nazi ranks, urged on by their officers, charged at our defences for the third time. And once again they got right up close to us, pelting our trenches with their long-handled grenades. But few of them produced the result desired by the Germans; we contrived to catch the grenades in the air or pick them up from the trench floor and toss them back.

Dashing from one firing position to another, from one platoon to another, I helped the troops to deal with the Nazis with the fire from my sniper's rifle. One after another I put their officers out of commission and helped to defuse tense situations which arose right by the trenches. Left without any officers, the German soldiers lost their heads; with nobody to urge them on, they did not know what to do – whether to keep going forward straight into our bullets or to turn back. And of course they chose the latter. With hesitating soldiers our troops and machine gunners knew only too well what to do. They calmly picked off the Nazis as they dashed all over the place.

Moving like this along the trench, I ended up at the company command post. I wanted the company commander, Lieutenant Popov, to allow observers to take up a position right on the railway embankment. This would allow us an excellent view of what was happening in the Nazi camp and enable us, at least for a few minutes, to find out about the enemy's intentions. But there turned out to be no commanding officer at the command point.

'He's with the platoons,' said Health Instructor Anatoly Knyazev.

'But we have no contact with the platoons – the line seems to be broken in several places,' added telephonist Kiriyanov. 'Where to look for him now, I can't imagine!' And, dashing through the door of the dugout, he added on the run: 'I'm going to look for the break; maybe I'll find the commander – the 1st Battalion were asking for him . . .'

A couple of minutes after his departure we saw about a dozen enemy bombers approaching our defences. Circling above, they dropped like a stone and began swooping on the trenches.

'Air attack!' cried the lookouts, and in a moment all the firing sites were empty. Our troops had hidden in their foxholes. Those of us at the command post remained standing by the dugout door, also ready any second to dive for cover, and continued to observe the course of events, apprehensive only of a direct hit.

Detaching themselves from the planes were some black droplets, which kept increasing in size and threatened in a second to turn our dugouts and our already churned up trenches into a heap of ruins. But on this occasion nothing fearful happened; apparently unsure of the environment in the sector, the Nazi pilots dropped their lethal load untidily, a little bit behind our trenches. Whether it was because they thought that the gully and trenches were already occupied by their own soldiers, or were afraid of the fire from Semyon Yushin's AA battery, after two sorties the aircraft went on their way. However, there was still groaning and crashing all around, the earth continued to tremble and shake. Heavy lumps of earth tossed up high into the sky by exploding bombs crashed down where the 3rd Platoon was stationed.

I had seen many deaths over a year of war, but one of those has stayed in my memory to this day on account of its uselessness. Our Party organiser, Sergeant Pyotr Derevyanko, a favourite of the battalion, was killed before my very eyes by a direct shell hit during an artillery attack. He always turned up where he was needed. A mere 23-year-old, Pyotr never even considered the possibility that he would be killed. 'You and I have still not done anything for victory over the enemy; it's too early for us to die. We still have to visit Berlin,' he would tell the troops, inspiring them with confidence in their own strength. He also inspired me with the same idea. He loved life, and loved and understood people.

And now our Pyotr was gone . . We had only just been talking at the company command post, as we waited out the bombing raid. As soon as it had finished, Pyotr would not wait another minute. 'I'm off to the 3rd platoon. Seems they're having a hard time there.'

He had barely managed to run to the 2nd Platoon and was standing and talking to one of the troops, when suddenly the bombing raid was followed by an artillery bombardment. The second shell to fall in the platoon's position exploded at Pyotr's feet. When I reached the 2nd Platoon after the bombardment, it was all over; on the spot where Derevyanko and the soldier had been standing yawned a huge shell-hole . . .

But there was no time for grief. The war was still on.

'Has he got through, taken cover or is he dead?' we wondered, concerned about the telephone operator, who had still not returned to the command post.

'He didn't get through!' said radio operator Sergei Aksyonov for the umpteenth time. 'There's no contact!' he said, continuing to crank the handle of the hopelessly silent telephone set.

At this moment the earth began to tremble and shake again – the Germans had launched a new bombardment on our trenches. Under the cover of the artillery fire, right behind the exploding shells, the Nazis had again appeared in the gully. Bawling something as they went, they were approaching quickly, blazing away with machine guns loaded with explosive bullets. The noise all around was unimaginable, but the efforts of the Nazis made no impact on the experienced, battle-hardened Red Army troops – I saw how quickly our soldiers took up their positions.

Amidst the dust of the advance and the frenzied rattling of their machine guns, the Germans paid no attention to my shots at their back and did not even notice the dugout itself – the company command post was behind them, being situated in the railway embankment. They charged forward, still with the hope of overcoming the Russian trenches which had been inaccessible to them. Our command post and the three of us – myself, medical orderly Knyazev and radio-operator Aksyonov – thus ended up not only cut off from the company, but without any contact with the platoons. Ammunition was nearly gone; the cartridges in my possession and a few grenades – that was all we had at our disposal.

'Yes, our arsenal's not exactly overstocked, lads! But never mind, we'll stick it out! I'm sure they'll come to our rescue. And not just us, but the company in general!' I tried to cheer up my comrades, and also reassure myself. 'But we'll still hold the command post!'

I was not wrong; battalion commander Arkhipov sent out all the battalion snipers to help us and reinforced the company with a platoon of machine gunners, who were under the command of Sergeant Karpov, both a sniper and a competent machine gunner. The battalion commander concentrated almost all the firepower at his disposal on the sector. And from our rear the regimental artillery and Semyon Yushin's AA battery again bombarded the gully. But we only found out about this later. In the meantime, we needed to decide what we ourselves were to do.

Through cracks in the dugout door I could see almost the entire gully through which the Nazis were now running towards the trenches, while, through a small window, our defences were easily visible. Just as before, there was a large number of Nazis.

'Get the grenades ready!' I shouted to Anatoly Knyazev, breaking the window with my rifle butt. 'I'll help the lads right from here! But use the grenades to stop the Nazis getting close to the dugout, guard the entrance! Sergei, keep trying to get the radio going – it doesn't look as if there'll be any more artillery strikes. Try to get the door open – Knyazev will help you.'

I fired shot after shot into the backs of the attacking Nazis. For the time being it was easy; the Nazis could not see me and could not hear my shots. But they did not only fall from my bullets – I could see only too well how our troops were fighting off the Nazis. 'So long as they have some officers there still alive, even just one!' I thought, reloading my rifle for the umpteenth time.

Knyazev, who had long exhausted all the cartridges in his Nagant revolver except the three left 'for emergencies', as he put it, was following my firing and prompting me:

'There, to the left, there's an officer, waving his arms. He's about to jump into the trench. Get him!' he cried and in an instant I subdued the overzealous Nazi. And each time yet another German fell dead from my bullet, Anatoly would keep count, amusingly adding comments:

'That's the twelfth one played out! Number seventeen has waved goodbye! Number twenty has ascended to the heavens!'

Amidst the feverish firing and the excitement of battle I failed to notice that I was beginning to make audible comments myself just before dispatching the next Nazi: 'Well, pray to God! Thine be the kingdom, bastard!' And, again setting my sights on yet another Nazi, I would smoothly press the trigger with words: 'Gone to your maker, swine!' However, coming to my senses, I told Knyazev: 'Listen, quit that racket right under my nose. You'll never be able to count them all anyway. Better to do something useful – help Sergei to get the door open! Or else we won't be able to get out of here if anything happens!'

Aksyonov had long been trying to open the dugout door, but to no avail; it was jammed by the body of a Nazi whom Knyazev had felled with a point-blank pistol shot through the crack in the door. Knyazev went to help Sergei and the door finally gave way. Aksyonov slipped out, taking several hand-grenades with him and the torn-off end of the telephone wire. Sergei was not away for long. He had just managed to connect the ends of the wire, which had been broken by a shell, before the telephone began to buzz.

Knyazev went and picked up the receiver.

'Hallo, hallo! "Daisy"! Why don't you speak? It's the 3rd Battalion speaking. What's happening with you? Can you hear me? Report on your situation immediately!'

'The "Third" is asking about your situation!' said Knyazev, glancing at me. 'It's the head of the battalion general staff ringing!' he added, to make it sound more convincing.

'Well, report, then! Don't you know what to say, or what? Then say that . . .' But I was unable to finish the sentence before Aksyonov whizzed into dugout like a bullet. Several explosions could be heard behind him.

'They've started firing again, the dirty wretches! Well, how are things? All in order? Working again?' And he grabbed the telephone receiver from Knyazev. 'Comrade "Third"! Radio operator Aksyonov reporting. The telephone operator has been killed. I've only just restored contact. There are three of us at the command post: sniper Nikolaev, medical orderly Knyazev and me. We are fighting off the Germans. They're rolling towards us, aiming for the company trenches . . .'

'Say that we're requesting artillery fire at ourselves! Get them to strike harder at the gully! There are so many, we'll never shoot them all,' I prompted Aksyonov.

'Comrade "Third"! Comrade Nikolaev requests shelling of the gully, and let them fire directly at the command post! Only quickly! The Germans may break into the dugout! There are a lot of them and they're pelting the trenches with grenades. Nikolaev is shooting them through the window.'

'Got you. Where's the company commander?'

'We don't know. He went to see the company straight after the bombing raid. We have no contact with the platoons and it's impossible to restore it – there are Germans all around. We can't get out of the dugout. Hurry up and fire!'

'Just hang on and we'll give them what for! Don't leave the dugout. You'll have to adjust our range from there!'

The shell and mortar explosions drowned out the voice from the general staff – our artillery had begun to strike the gully.

'Excellent, "Third", excellent! Thanks for the fireworks! Now aim a little bit farther forward, about fifty metres, towards the embankment. The Germans are running in our direction, towards the command post! Don't worry about us. Aim at the dugout!' Aksyonov shouted down the telephone receiver.

I fired at the Nazis, who were now retreating in fear – right into their faces. Over the gully darkness was thickening and visibility had grown noticeably worse.

'Twenty-eight!' Knyazev continued counting my hits. 'Well, it looks like that's the last for the day, eh? And, indeed, silence hung over the gully. The firing had ceased on both sides. The Germans had pulled back and the previous situation was restored. They would not bother us at night, of this we were certain.

Sometimes in war a single battle, even one lasting a few minutes, can stick in the memory for the rest of your life. In battles like this the young turn grey, the quiet ones become bold, the insolent turn out to be cowards. In battles like this not only are people found out, but you find out about yourself. This battle went on almost the whole day. I realised that I was not afraid of the Germans at all, even if they outnumbered us ten-fold, because I was not alone; I had my comrades beside me and they would always bail me out at a difficult moment. And Nazis had to be annihilated if I wanted to survive myself and prevent my friends from perishing.

When silence fell, I felt how terribly tired I was, how great the tension had been. I felt like sitting down, stretching out my legs to still the repulsive nervous tremble affecting my knees.

'Aksyonov, go back with Knyazev to the company, at the double! Restore communications with them and help the wounded. I'll look after the telephone. Make sure you find the company commander. If he's alive, he can go back to the command post, to the telephone,' I said, wiping the sweat from my face with my cap.

The lads were out of the dugout in an instant and back in our trenches within a minute. At moments like this it is important that somebody should take charge in an authoritative way. For them I was now that authority, though only in terms of my title. I also needed the company commander to sort me out so I would not grow limp from fatigue. I was already feeling sleepy. At the command post I was completely on my own.

Sometime later, after the lads had withdrawn to the dugout, the telephone buzzed. I picked up the receiver.

'How are things there, Nikolaev? What can you see in front of you?' asked the 'Third' after I had identified myself and reported on the situation.

'Peace and quiet over here,' I reported. 'The Germans have gone back to their starting position and may not bother us till the morning. I'm on my own at the command post, waiting for the company commander. I've sent the medical orderly and the radio operator back to the company – to restore communication and find the lieutenant.'

'Good. If there's anything new, report immediately. If Popov turns up, let him contact me at once,' ordered Captain Naida.

About twenty minutes after this conversation Anatoly Knyazev, who had returned to the company command post, was telling me: 'Well, it looks like the war's over for today. The company commander's still alive and he'll be here any minute. I saw your friends in the trenches – snipers Rakhmatullin and Dobrik.

I heard they gave the Nazis what for. Ivan Karpov also brought his machine-gun platoon and had his own rifle with him and was working a "double shift" as they say. But the main thing is that we got good back-up!'

Sniper Sergeant Ivan Karpov was known in the regiment to be an excellent machine gunner. As well as that he knew how to work with people; he could teach his subordinates how to shoot accurately.

They were great friends – Ivan Karpov and his Maxim. They could not bear being separated for long and they had bailed each other out a number of times. Ivan was there with his machine-gun today.

'Gee, it'd be nice to have dinner now!' said Karpov's partner and number two dreamily.

'You'll have to earn your dinner!' Ivan commented,' Let's build up the breastwork under the machine gun and clean up the firing position!' And the machine gunners routinely and smartly began to arrange the firing position. The work went well. It was quiet all around.

'Stop!' cried Sergeant Karpov suddenly.

A bullet whipped past close by, then another, while on the left flank of the company there was already an exchange of rifle and submachine-gun fire.

'Well, lads, smoko's over! Everyone to their stations, everyone disperse! Let's get ready to greet our uninvited guests,' came the directions from Karpov, but his troops had already manned the machine guns in any case. German mortar bombs were flying over their heads, exploding somewhere to the rear, behind the trenches.

'Bunglers!' somebody called out contemptuously with regard to the Nazi gunners. 'They should learn to shoot!'

'If I'd known, I wouldn't have bothered to duck!' another machine gunner echoed him. 'Now we'll show you how to shoot!'

The troops were joking. But as soon as the Nazis began to approach our trenches, having populated the entire gully, the machine gunners' faces became stern and concentrated, and their movements spare and decisive. As soon as the enemy were within twenty or thirty metres, the sergeant gave the order: 'Fire!'

The first to speak up was Karpov's Maxim. Its voice was loud, harsh and angry. 'Rat-tat-tat-tat!' Ivan blazed away at the Nazis. In response came the cries and groans of the wounded Fritzes, who had not expected such a decisive repulse. Under the impact of the machine-gun fire the attacking wave receded for a moment, but, gathering again, launched another headlong attack.

'You want more? Here it comes! What, you don't like it?' said Ivan Karpov, angrily squeezing out the words through firmly clenched teeth as he pressed the trigger.

The Nazi lines now halted, became confused and turned back. The Germans were fleeing, leaving dozens of bodies in the gully. There was a particularly large number in front of Sergeant Karpov's gun. But then enemy mortar bombs began exploding right in front of his firing position.

'Found me out, the rats!' said Ivan and carefully covered his machine gun with a waterproof cape. 'Rest up for a bit, mate!' He took up his sniper's rifle. 'Let them think they've smashed the machine gun!'

But the Germans kept up the pressure. More and more of them appeared from beyond the railway embankment. They approached, stooping low to the ground, encouraging themselves with the rattle of their submachine guns.

'Grenades at the ready, everybody!' shouted Sergeant Karpov, and carried on firing his machine-gun, going through one belt after another until the water in the barrel jacket boiled over. Beside him his ammunition bearer, Vasily Neznanov, was firing at the Nazis with his sniper's rifle.

'Six!' he called, counting his hits, but suddenly he groaned: 'That's it, lads, bye-bye! Sergeant write to my . . .' and, without finishing the sentence, he fell to the bottom of the trench.

Looking round at the dying man, Karpov only wavered a second. Then he leapt down to him and seized the sniper's rifle from his already chilled hands. He had no time to shake his comrade's hand and bid him farewell. He merely gritted his teeth even more firmly, straightened up the stones on which the machine-gun was resting, lowered the sights and called out, looking straight ahead:

'We'll avenge you, Vasily!'

And he began to shoot the Nazis with even greater fury.

Suddenly there was a violent shockwave, which knocked Karpov away from his machine-gun.

'A mortar! Bastard! But where's the machine-gun?'

And overcoming the dull pain and oncoming nausea and dizziness, he dashed towards his Maxim which enemy hands were already reaching out for from beyond the parapet. One rifle shot, one cry from a dead Nazi – and the hands were gone. Manoeuvring himself into position, Karpov threw three grenades over the parapet one after the other, and, clinging to the trench wall, caught the sound of the earth shuddering and swaying beyond the trench followed by the cries of the wounded Nazis.

Like Ivan, his troops began to toss grenades at the Nazis. And this time the machine gunners did not allow the enemy to burst into our trenches.

'We haven't done a bad job together, mate!' said Ivan, patting the machine gun and only now did he breathe a deep sigh of relief. Then, taking advantage of a lull, as one of his occasional jokes, he rapped out the folk-dance tune 'Barynya' with bursts of his machine gun.

The troops in the trenches smiled; it meant he was alive, Ivan Karpov and his Maxim!

Karpov was in love with his machine gun. During the lulls between battles he would take some oiled oakum, clean his Maxim and talk to it as if it were a good friend.

'It's damp outside, so I'll give you a good coating of oil now.'

And the sergeant's face – broad, sharp-chinned, obstinate and determined – adopted an expression of deep concern. His bright eyes lit up warmly when he was working on the jet-black steel of a machine-gun, banishing every cloudy thought . . .

We were into the second day. For a while it was quiet everywhere; the firing had fallen silent on both sides. But we were sure that the Germans would not abandon their attempt to break through to Leningrad so easily. And in the meantime, taking advantage of the lull, the handful of troops remaining from the company strove to put their defences in order and got ready to repel enemy attacks. Ammunition was brought up from the rear, new foxholes were dug; these had been so effective in saving troops from the bombing and shelling. Only a direct hit on a foxhole could bury a soldier alive, but the chances of this were almost nil.

Three more times over these twenty-four hours, hordes of Nazis charged our trenches, but each time they were forced to retreat with heavy losses. Enraged by battle, our dirty, hungry and worn-out troops threw grenade after grenade after the retreating Germans. Towards the end of the day the remnants of our company, supported by their neighbours, were the first to break through on the heels of the enemy into their trenches beyond the railway embankment. Only one enemy firing point, situated on a small hill, failed to fall into our hands. It sprayed the counter-attacking battalion with machine-gun bullets. The advance on our front threatened to come to a halt.

It was then that regimental commissar Colonel Tomlyonov appeared in our trenches. He had recently joined the regiment in place of our Ivan Ilyich Agashin, who had been recalled to the HQ of the Leningrad Front border forces. We still did not know Commissar Tomlyonov very well, but we liked the way he came to the trenches before the battle and simply said: 'Follow me, lads! Communists forward!' And he crawled across the wet grass, drawing the rest after him.

It was not their second, but probably about their tenth wind that our troops got up again for a counter-attack. And it came off! We occupied the enemy trenches. The machine gun which had been hindering our advance was knocked out – someone contrived to use his helmet to cover the slit of the gun-port which was belching out the torrent of lead. A grenade tossed straight after into the communication trench finished the job – three Germans emerged from the depths of the position and walked along the trench with their hands raised high. The fearsome enemy pillbox had fallen silent. But not for long. After a while it started up again; however, the impenetrable steel fortress was now firing in the opposite direction. It was in reliable hands. Behind the armour plating of the skilfully camouflaged tank buried in the ground there now sat Soviet snipers and observers. Now we had to defend the positions seized from the Germans. Defend them whatever the cost.

Our advance halted for a while – the Germans had still not recovered from the defeat, while we were occupying new trenches, in which the firing positions had to be urgently reconstructed after being turned in the opposite direction, towards the enemy.

Our troops looked in the German dugouts, which till quite recently had been solid, spacious, and comfortable and were now churned up by the explosions of our anti-tank grenades. They did not venture in; there were lots of lice and the dugouts stank of burnt sulphur, gunpowder . . . and something very alien and unpleasant.

I went into one of them. Some rags were scattered about: women's underwear, old domestic equipment, children's toys. Leftover food, photographs and letters were strewn around. I picked up an unopened letter from the floor. It was from Dortmund. 'Kurt has sent blankets and various things from Russia,' I read, barely making out some *Frau*'s scrawl. Mama was urging her son Hans to loot and kill. But her Hansie would not be sending anything from Russia – he was lying in a trench covered with lice . . .

With a feeling of disgust and loathing I left the dugout, but was not able to deny myself the pleasure of kicking the dead Nazi. 'What are you lying there for, ratbag? You can stay lying! Soon you'll all be lying like that!'

However, infuriated by their setbacks, the Nazis did not rest. Our watchmen reported that the Germans were assembling again, this time for a counter-attack.

Now the German submachine gunners were storming their own former trenches. But our gunners and Yushin's AA crew had long been seeking to find their range in this area! And I was conveniently ensconced in the turret of the German tank – my sniper's rifle was already hot from continuous firing.

I was glad about the convenient position, glad that more and more Nazis were dropping from my bullets, and I was concerned only for my comrades, who were also conducting sniper fire from somewhere close by. 'How have they set themselves up? Are they safe? Are they alive?' I was not worried about Ivan Karpov, Ivan Dobrik and Zagid Rakhmatullin – they were experienced guys; they would not come unstuck. But what about the others? Those who had only recently learned the sniper's art and had barely managed to open their tally of vengeance?

A sniper in defence is a big plus. For a good commanding officer the snipers in a detachment occupy a special place and he has a particular concern for them. A competent commander is not only concerned about increasing the ranks of new snipers, but he also creates the necessary conditions for them, helps them in their work and cares about their safety. A commander like this will not send a top-class sniper into a bayonet charge – he knows that in this case a sniper will be of greater use shooting from a well-camouflaged firing position, supporting the attack. There are occasions when well-positioned snipers can bring success to the detachment in battle and sometimes decide the outcome of the attack itself.

Yesterday had shown that the outcome of the battle was determined mainly by the dead-eyed fire of the snipers, who did not let the enemy near their trenches. Many of them wiped out up to ten or more Nazis in the engagement. Besides, it was not just the quantity but, so to speak, the quality of the felled enemy. The snipers annihilated officers, artillery spotters, machine gunners, sentries and those soldiers who were on the point of leaping into our trenches.

We firmly held on to the captured territory. In the course of a short summer night the troops managed to re-equip the German trenches once again, and in the morning, when the sun rose, the waking Germans saw that a new, inaccessible barrier had sprung up before their very eyes. A streak of ill-luck had set in for the enemy. But the fiendish enemy did not slacken. Deep into the night our troops beat off attack after attack and the number of Nazi dead rose. We had almost no casualties.

We spent the following night in relative calm. The Germans were afraid of the dark; they would not fight at night. They sent flares into the black sky one after another, in anticipation of an assault from us. But we did not attempt to attack; we had to rest, put our defences into order. Only the snipers were firing – at Nazi silhouettes showing up against the glow of the flares.

On the third morning the Germans again attempted to restore the situation. Their objective was now much more modest – to chase us out of an advantageous site and return to their trenches. The battlefield was filled with the sound of crashing and clanking – enemy tanks had emerged from a ravine accompanied by infantry and were heading for our front line. Their guns were belching out shell after shell as they went, tossing up fountains of soil over our heads. And again our dreaded orchestra of mortars and artillery struck up. The fire of our riflemen and snipers cut off the infantry from the tanks, and the armour-plated juggernauts turned back, pursued by the fire of our guns.

Their aircraft did not bring the Germans success either; as soon as four Stukas appeared overhead, Yushin's AA crew unleashed a hurricane of fire. The German pilots hastened to drop their bombs ... on their own front line. One of the planes was shot down. It exploded before it hit the ground and the fragments sprayed over the Nazis. The Nazis failed to achieve anything on the third day either. Their plans were frustrated by the steadfastness of our troops, the skilful direction of our commanders, the activity of the regimental political staff, and the personal example of those who encouraged the Red Army men on to notable feats.

After a few days the battalion held a Party meeting at which the results of the three-day engagement with the Nazis were summed up. At the end of the meeting regimental commissar Tomlyonov said: 'And now have a read of this.' And he held out several issues of a newspaper. It was our army four-column paper *Striking the Enemy*.

I took one of the newspapers myself. In the first column my eyes were immediately attracted by a headline in bold type: 'Deputy political instructor Nikolaev has wiped out 211 enemies of our homeland!' And a little below, in smaller type: 'Follow his example, multiply the tally of sacred vengeance!' Featured here was my portrait, along with the caption: 'The Military Council extends greetings to sniper Nikolaev.' My heart began beating loudly. I started reading the text, but the letters were swimming before my eyes:

> Dear Comrade Nikolaev! The Military Council warmly congratulates you on the annihilation of Nazi criminals in recent battles for the city of Lenin. Having wiped out 211 Nazis, you have shown in action your selfless love for your homeland and your fierce hatred for the Nazi monsters.
>
> We wish you further success in the great and noble cause of cleansing the Soviet land from the German invaders.

And the signature read: 'Military Council of the Army'.

Tearing myself away from the newspaper, I glanced stupefied at the troops around me – the eyes of my smiling friends were looking at me.

'What have we got here? Take a look!' said Ivan Dobrik in a mixture of Russian and Ukrainian, holding out another newspaper, this a national one.

I took it with trembling hands. It was *Pravda*.

'From the Soviet Information Bureau,' I read. And then the headline: 'In three days, sniper Nikolaev wiped out 104 Nazis'. A correspondent I was unfamiliar with named N. Voronov was relating 'some details about the military operations of this master of sharp-shooting.'

'And here's *Izvestiya*: it's got the stuff from the Soviet Information Bureau, and there's a letter from Master Bushtyrkov – from the Kirov works; we were there in May at a celebration. Here he is writing to Yevgeni . . . '

> From the people of Leningrad to sniper Nikolaev. Leningrad Front, 10 August (TASS special correspondent). Sniper Nikolaev of the . . . detachment, who, as has been already reported in the press, wiped out 104 Nazis in three days, is the recipient of numerous letters voicing warm greetings and congratulations from the working people of the city of Leningrad. Decorated master Bushtyrkov, from one of the factories, addresses the sniper as follows: 'I have learned about your unprecedented feat. It is, my dear soldier, a great achievement. Greetings to you and thanks. We remember the winter, dear Comrade Nikolaev, we remember the whole of this grim year, and we know that the enemy will pay for it all – for all the destruction and suffering. Keep hitting them, my dear fellow, keep hitting the Germans as you have over these three days. Instruct your comrades in your high level of expertise, in the art of the sniper. May our Red Army have thousands, tens and hundreds of thousands of people like you.

'It's correct what the man writes,' said the commissar. 'Instructing others – that's our joint objective!'

And, taking a slender school exercise book from a clipboard, the commissar held it out to me, adding:

'If I were you, Nikolaev, I would immediately write a reply to the greetings of the Army Military Council.'

'True, Comrade Commissar. Only it's a difficult task!'

'Well, let's sit down and think it all out together. You've got friends here to help you, as always . . .'

This is what we came up with:

I have received your letter. I am deeply moved by the attention you have paid to me. It inspires me to new feats. I have wiped out 211 Nazis. My operations will not be limited by that. As long as my heart beats, as long as my hands can hold a rifle, and my eyes can see, I will go on annihilating the brown plague. My pledge, given at the front-line rally of snipers – to wipe out 300 Nazis – will be honourably fulfilled. I have passed on and will continue to pass on my experience of operations to broad masses of Red Army troops and I will rear new snipers. I call on all snipers on our front to strike at the enemy with even greater hatred, to ensure that not a single Nazi remains alive on our land.

Let us promote the spread of sniping more broadly.

Let us have more military competition between detachments!

Military greetings from decorated sniper, deputy political instructor Y. Nikolaev.

The commissar took the letter, carefully folded it, put it in his field bag and slammed it shut as if placing a full-stop after a question now resolved. Then, saying farewell to everyone, as he left he told me curtly:

'Report with Dobrik at the regimental staff headquarters tomorrow – there'll be a meeting. We'll let you know the time later. Well, comrades, I wish you all the same success in wiping out the Nazi scum. Three hundred and four Nazis were killed in this three-day engagement by our snipers alone. May the tally of vengeance for each of you grow from day to day, so they write about you in the newspapers and mention you in Soviet Information Bureau despatches.'

'Nikolaev, have you read the letter from your mother?' Ivan Karpov suddenly asked me.

'No, I haven't seen any letter.'

'How come? Who's got Yevgeni's letter from his mother?'

'Here it is! Only the letter arrived without an envelope.' And Zagid Rakhmatullin handed over a newspaper folded in four.

In the first column of the newspaper *For the Motherland* I read the headline: 'Hit them harder, son!' and in small print at the side:

Letter to renowned sniper of our front, Y. Nikolaev, from his mother in Tambov.

> My dear Yevgeni! I am proud of you, of your success in battle, when you despatched 104 Nazi ratbags in three days. Go after them, son! As long as your heart beats in your breast and your hands can hold a rifle. Avenge all the sisters, brothers, and children who have perished at the hands of those bloodthirsty reptiles. I am waiting for you, son, to come home after victory! All our family send you greetings and best wishes for success in battle. Love and kisses! Your mother. Greetings to your comrades in arms.

'How did she find out? I didn't write anything to her,' I said, surprised.

'From the newspapers. You don't think she doesn't read them, do you?' Ivan Karpov suggested. 'Well, let's get back to our stations, lads; the meeting's over. Let's carry on with our work – we need to justify what we said and promised today!'

And he was the first to set off through the trenches to his platoon. The others followed him, stubbing out their roll-your-own cigarettes.

# 19.

# Such is our Work

The defenders of Leningrad achieved a truly legendary feat. They showed unparalleled examples of staunchness and doggedness, a high degree of awareness, self-sacrifice, patriotism and fearlessness in battle in the name of the freedom and happiness of their people. Without in any way understating the significance in positional warfare of artillery, tanks, aircraft and the navy, which did a lot on the Leningrad Front during the early years of the war, it needs to be said that the main role in the defence was nevertheless performed by the infantry – soldiers with rifles who faced the enemy head on and stopped him under the walls of the city.

In the autumn of 1941, at the most testing time in the defence of Leningrad, a snipers' movement was born in the forces of the Leningrad Front; its initiators were army Communist Party and Young Communist League members. Adopted in good time by the political workers and commanders of various units and formations, this movement had by the beginning of 1942, acquired a truly massive scale. Whether operating in defence or fighting aggressive or defensive battles, Soviet snipers struck at the Nazi invaders with equal success.

Every one of our shots was greed by a hurricane of fire. And at the same time every shell, every cartridge, had to be accounted for:

ammunition was in short supply . . And yet if, in the early months of war, the Nazis walked around their positions upright and felt like lords of a conquered land, with the advent of our snipers, the situation changed sharply – the Nazis were forced not just to run stooping closer and closer to the ground, but literally to crawl along it. Our land was becoming too hot for them to stand on.

'The Russians fire with diabolical accuracy; all their shots are at the head, between the eyes or in the neck. On quiet days, Russian snipers were knocking out six to ten men from my company,' one of the Nazi prisoners testified at the time. According to the prisoners' narratives, there were even rumours among enemy soldiers that a special unit of Siberian hunters had come to Leningrad who could hit a squirrel in the eye.

The sniper movement energised our defence, saved soldiers from the dangerous immobility of trench warfare and opened up the opportunity to inflict significant losses on the enemy with limited means. Snipers had existed as military formations in army units since before the war. During the war these super-sharpshooters became instructors of sniper schools in their units, operated as rank and file snipers and were the first to open the tally of vengeance.

On 26 January 1942, the Military Council of the Leningrad Front informed the Central Committee of the Communist Party that, as of 20 January 1942, the snipers' ranks included over 4,200 soldiers, officers and political staff. In the first twenty days of 1942 snipers of the Twenty-Third, Forty-Second and Fifty-Fifth Armies and the Maritime Pacific Operational Group had annihilated more than 7,000 enemy officers and men. By 22 February 1942, the snipers' ranks had been increased to 6,000.

We snipers strove to select firing positions where the Germans least expected them. I, for example, often set myself up in the ruins of a building, behind a stove chimney, and fired through the broken door of the stove itself. I fired from tall trees, from the bell towers of church ruins. I would at times get up quite close to the German trenches and, camouflaged under a bush, lie motionless almost in full view of the Germans, taking one or two shots only when the German or our own artillery was rumbling, or during exchanges of machine-gun fire. It was particularly convenient to fire from a tank that had been put out of action; inside it, you were completely safe, your shots were inaudible, and you did not have to worry about enemy shrapnel or bullets. For a sniper camouflage is a great thing!

We had to operate through all the hours of daylight. At night as a rule we were off duty. But long before first light we were already in our observation points. Whether standing in a trench, in a site earlier equipped for shooting, or lying camouflaged in no man's land, we kept watch on the enemy defences, which we knew like the back of our hand. Indeed, how could it be otherwise? The slightest change in the relief of the locality and its outlines was instantly spotted. Every barely noticeable blade of grass, any object falling within our field of vision, was thoroughly scrutinised. And the discovery of something new, at times completely insignificant, in the enemy defences, instantly put us on alert. One day some kind of stick appeared in the enemy trenches. It had not been there the day before, or earlier. What could it mean? Was an ordinary sighting telescope mounted in this twig-like stick? And was there a Nazi spotter or sniper concealed there? Daily activities like this sharpened your vision and hearing and made you more quick-witted. They taught you to camouflage yourself skilfully, to anticipate the enemy's cunning plans in time and, correspondingly, to deceive him ingeniously yourself, and to set traps for Nazi observers and snipers.

We reported the results of our observations every day to those in command and they used our information like scouts' reports. We let them know about new, well-camouflaged firing positions, dugouts, and firing and observation points and used tracer bullets to indicate these targets to artillery spotters. It only took two or three shells and there would be nothing left of a firing station.

No question, a sniper's work is dangerous and very laborious: just try lying for a day almost without moving under the rays of a baking sun, or in a downpour, in a snowstorm, or frost, and also perhaps in the sights of a Nazi sniper. It is far from easy. Especially if you have taken part in hand-to-hand combat the day before and you have still not recovered from it, not rested, not slept enough and you are hungry to boot. All the same we persisted in doing our job, striving to wipe out as many of the Nazi scum as we could.

To this day I remember my pupils – Senior Sergeant Pyotr Derevyanko, Privates Vasily Mushtakov, Anatoly Vinogradov, Solovyov, Ryakhin, Dyakov, Zosya Mitskevich and the others. There were about fifty of them and they wiped out over 600 Nazis. And how could I forget our 'International' – Ukrainian sniper Ivan Dobrik, Byelorussian Vasily Shevchenko, the Tartar Zagid Rakhmatullin, the Russian lads Ivan Karpov, Vladimir Shubin, Sergei Dmitriev, Valentin Loktyev, Nikolai Kachalin, Vladimir Dudin, Yuri Semyonov, Ivan Vasilyev, the old schoolteacher Pugin, and other regimental mates.

And our girls – Maria Mitrofanova (now Barskova), Maria Nazarov, Margarita Katikovskaya, and others, who lay in ambush with a sniper's rifle and patiently endured all the adversities and burdens of war? For them, as for us, there was no carefree youth and the only joy was that of seeing the tally of vengeance grow.

At the end of 1942 I was transferred to counter-intelligence and my sniper's score was cut off at the total of 324. I had nevertheless kept the pledge I had given to Andrey Alexandrovich Zhdanov and all those present at the first rally of snipers at the Smolny. Having liberated Leningrad from the enemy siege, our division, along with other units of the Leningrad Front, pressed forward, drove the Nazis back and reached their actual den. Travelling the entire route with me was my sniper's rifle, the butt of which still bears the three large, two medium-sized and four small stars traced on it during the war years . . .

# 20.

# Thirty-Five Years Later

So there I was with a new job. I was promoted to rank of senior lieutenant and a position in the security department of the counter-intelligence agency *Smersh*.

I had commenced my new duties in my old division, in one of its regiments, where I served two battalions at once; there were not enough security staff at the time. It was still on the same front line, with the same shell-torn trenches and, in front of us, the same battered town of Uritsk, occupied by the Nazis. And still the same exhausting daily air raids, shelling and the same old whistle of enemy bullets overhead.

My main responsibility in the regiment was to help those in command to fulfil their objective, and to ensure the timely apprehension and disarming of enemy agents. For this I had to have an excellent knowledge of every soldier and officer in my two battalions. But then I was transferred to the 96th Howitzer Artillery Brigade of the 23rd Artillery Division, which was stationed by the Pulkovo Heights. I enjoyed being with the brigade. The gunners were intelligent people, cultured, highly literate and battle-keen, and there were many Communist Party and Young Communist League members among them. Working with people like that was easy and uncomplicated.

Gunners who were brigade scouts walked through our firing positions to the forward defence line. I liked their commander, a very tall, extraordinarily appealing and jolly young officer named Sergei Shornikov. He was a legend in the brigade; everyone knew him. What did I know about him? He was from Moscow and he had finished college. He was a determined, courageous and extremely good-natured fellow, with no pretensions. Though covered in well-deserved military glory, he did not in the slightest revel in it. It was very easy not just to get to know him, but to get close to him. We became friends when Sergei was appointed commander of the 1st Battalion. At that time our forces had already begun to drive the Nazis back.

On route marches the battalion commander travelled ahead in a staff car with the head of the divisional staff, Captain Polozov. Gherman Polozov was like his commanding officer. Together they formed a single unit, somehow complementing each other. The only thing that distinguished the chief of staff from the divisional commander was his height – 1 metre 60, like me! Neither was short of a word, and they were both lively, smart and cheery. I usually travelled in the middle of the column, while the deputy political instructor brought up the rear. At halts we all assembled at the staff vehicle. There we would consult, eat and relax. The battalion's deputy commander for political affairs, Yefim Zakharovich Klimovich, who had been called up from the reserves, was twice as old as any of us. Mild by character, a good family man from the Far East, he loved life, loved people and felt for them, but at work he was a true commissar – solicitous, attentive and kind. But Major Klimovich perished in an appallingly inept way. It happened at the beginning of April 1944 somewhere near Pskov or Ostrov. We had been making good progress, but the advance had halted and the battalion was given the chance to rest and put men and equipment in order. We were waiting for the provisions truck to arrive with its kitchen and our dinner. We had stopped in an exposed place. Flowing past not far away was a small stream or, rather, a creek. Someone wanted to build some defence works on this bare patch but had not finished the job. There were no trenches of any dimension, but in places the land had been hollowed out seemingly with a view to constructing dugouts. They were three metres by three metres in area and of the same depth.

With Major Klimovich present I was in the vehicle interrogating a Nazi scout we had only just detained. And suddenly somewhere far away, and then closer and closer, exploding shells could be heard. It was at this point I heard the voice of the radio operator:

'Comrade Captain, artillery fire! Get out of the vehicle and take cover!'

Being outside, he understood the situation clearly. But I had not had time to gather up the documents before a shell exploded overhead and, with a frightful hoarse wheeze, the mortally wounded Klimovich collapsed onto the floor. Still sitting there with a huge shell fragment in his temple, the spy had also fallen silent for eternity. My overcoat, which was hanging on a nail at the head of the bed, was also shredded by numerous fragments . . . I leapt out of the vehicle and dashed to where everybody else was running – to the hollow covered with a waterproof cape and used as a temporary dugout. I jumped down and with some difficulty thrust myself into a corner. 'Quite a crowd . . . ' was all I could think before a shell fell into this hollow followed by the boom of an explosion.

What happened next I was told ten days later. It was like this. As soon as the bombardment finished (apparently there was a Nazi spotter sitting somewhere nearby), our medical orderlies began to offer medical assistance to the wounded. They ran to the hollow, which had been churned up by the explosion, and saw there was nobody to rescue . . . They decided to fill it in, turning it into a communal grave.

The April soil was hard, frozen and slightly dusted with snow. Digging was difficult. I don't know what it was actually like, but this was what I heard: tossing in yet another spade-full of soil, someone shouted: 'Stop! There's somebody alive – he's moving!' Either the cold earth and snow came to my aid, or else I came to of my own accord and began to move around. It was then that a soldier noticed me. I was dragged out, covered in blood, laid on a stretcher, and dispatched to hospital.

I was always lucky. There were times when it seemed I was not supposed to have been wounded, but killed! But all turned out well. Imagine for example the following situation: I am sitting in my own, or somebody else's, dugout. All is quiet, but something prompts me to leave, though without any good reason. I leave. And, returning, I find the dugout destroyed by a direct hit. And that happened several times. I think what preserved me was the love of my mother . . .

One day Sergei Shornikov brought along from somewhere a beautiful, huge motor bike without a side-car but a full tank of petrol.

'Get on! I'll take you for a ride,' he offered. 'You're not afraid of riding with the wind, are you?'

It was early morning and, after the rain, the air was fresh and warm, and the broad highway was empty and in excellent condition. Why not go for a ride? By now a crowd of idlers were making their feelings known: Shornikov was the reckless type; how about our boss? Would he chicken out or go?

But a voice inside me was already whispering: 'Don't get on, find some excuse!'. But there was no excuse to be found. We were off duty, there was no shelling, and there were no enemy in the vicinity . . .

'Let's go,' I said. 'Give her all she's got! I'll climb on behind you.'

Sergei tore off like a rocket. I knew that he was a classy driver of any make of automobile – I had been with him as a passenger. But I did not know that he could ride a motorbike. Now I was convinced and, in a nice sort of way, I envied Sergei: 'Well, blow me down, he does know how!'

No doubt about it, he was an excellent racer. We flew like an arrow along the smooth surface of what was a first-rate highway, and Sergei extracted from the vehicle everything it was capable of. I sat gripping Sergei's belt and behind his broad back I could not see what was happening ahead. And ahead was a huge shell-hole across which a temporary wooden bridge had been built. Its wide, smoothly planed boards were now damp from the rain.

Without reducing speed, Sergei tried to dash over the bridge, but he miscalculated, failed to consider that the bridge was damp. I came off the motor-bike, was tossed up three or four metres, and ended up in an empty field. Having flown about ten metres through the air, I crashed down right on top of Shornikov, who was already lying under the motor-bike. All this took place in an instant.

The highway was deserted; there was nobody to help. And Sergei was pretty smashed up, all covered in blood, and urgently needed a tetanus injection.

'Get on. Let's go back,' said Sergei, his face puckering with the pain, having already checked the state of the bike.

We got back safely. Somebody immediately called for a doctor, who treated our injuries. Sergei was firing off witticisms as if nothing had happened.

'I look around, and there's our boss in flight! Flying well, and even chooses his own landing ground. And, guess what, he landed with amazing accuracy!'

Sergei quickly rose through the ranks. Starting off as head of brigade reconnaissance, before my very eyes he became battalion commander and then an artillery battalion commander. His chest was covered in medals. We finished the war together in Berlin and signed our names on the walls of the Reichstag.

Sergei Shornikov and I tramped a long way side by side along front-line roads. We liberated Leningrad from the enemy siege, cleared the Leningrad region of Nazis, as well as the Baltic, Poland, Germany, and the Karelian Isthmus. We took Riga, Tallinn, Danzig and other cities. Together we lived a life that was relatively short in terms of time, but packed with events. And only later, long after the war, when constantly contacting veterans of my own infantry division, did I think: how is it I forgot about the 96th Artillery Brigade, which was no less of a home to me? Recalling that Sergei

Shornikov was a Muscovite, I made inquiries in the Moscow address directory. But whether it was because my information about Shornikov was insufficient, or for some other reason, I got no reply. And so I regretfully abandoned attempts to find anyone from my artillery brigade.

On the eve of major public holidays, the familiar name Shornikov often flashed before my eyes. 'The commandant of the Moscow Kremlin, Lieutenant General S. S. Shornikov is to take the salute . . .' and so on. Who was this Shornikov? 'Maybe the father of our Sergei? But surely not him?' I thought.

Some time went by and then I received a package from Moscow. I read the return address: 'Moscow, Kremlin, Commandant's Office, Shornikov, S. S.' I felt my temperature rising and my hands began to tremble. Not because it was the commandant of the Kremlin, but because it was Sergei Shornikov! That's what it was . . .

'Greetings, friend! At last we've found you, our gallant former ops chief!,' wrote Shornikov. And at this point I suddenly realised that it was him, my former battalion commander, Sergei Shornikov – only he would address me like that. 'First of all I would like to "praise" you for conducting a vigorous search for us over these last thirty-five years and more, while we camouflaged ourselves so as to be impossible to find, although you only had to scribble a line to me in the Kremlin in 1967, and everything would have fallen into place.' Later in the letter he described how he had 'found my range', using gunners' terminology. It turned out that a veterans' committee for our brigade had existed for many years and they met almost every year either in Moscow or in Leningrad.

'But then Fayar Khairzamanov, your former orderly, incidentally, gave me a book called *The Watchword is Victory*. In the recollections of the commander of the 109th Division, Rodionov, and regimental commissar Agashin the divisional snipers are mentioned, including you. It mentioned where you now live and work. The rest was a matter of technology . . .'

The letter was lengthy and written in a clear hand. After my demobilisation, Sergei had left the brigade for the post of divisional head of reconnaissance (the division was in Kaliningrad). And after the division was disbanded he was deputy head of artillery general staff in the 36th Guards Rifle Corps. In 1950 he entered the Frunze military academy. Subsequent service took him to various units and various posts, and now he was commandant of the Moscow Kremlin. 'It looks like he's the only one from the entire division who is still serving in the army,' I thought.

At the end of the letter Sergei insistently invited me to call in when in Moscow, and gave his address and telephone number. On arriving in Moscow in 1981 I called the number I knew. 'Kremlin commandant Shornikov,' I heard the familiar voice over the receiver. Barely containing my excitement, I introduced myself.

In literally a few minutes I was in Sergei's arms in his Kremlin office. We kissed and . . . the intervening thirty-five years, old age, wounds, and everything else seemed to vanish – and there before me, at a massive table covered with numerous telephones, sat the same young, cheery, good-natured lad of old – Sergei Shornikov.

# 21.

# 'Russian's Amazing Story'

Every year I travel for treatment at a sanatorium on a free pass given to me by the military as a war invalid. In the middle of this break I am joined by my wife Tatyana; she cannot abandon our home and our grandchild for long.

In the autumn of 1977 I received a pass to travel to Khosta. I found a flat next to the sanatorium for Tatyana; I only had to cross the road. The weather on that occasion was not so good – it rained almost every day. Only before our very departure did it become sunny and warm.

'It's Murphy's law,' said Tatyana. 'Such lovely days and we have to leave. Let's take a trip up to Sochi?'

Tanya was born in Sochi. Everything there was dear to her heart, memorable and interesting. Both of us always enjoy these trips. This time we were wandering round the area where she spent her childhood, where she went to school. We were tired of course and dropped in to the Pearl Hotel café to rest our legs and have a bite to eat at the same time. The café was deserted; everybody was probably at the beach after so many days of foul weather.

Almost straight after us two other couples sat down. At one table sat a cheery young man and woman, while the other was occupied by two middle-aged men. The men were talking loudly in a language that was unfamiliar to me.

'Why are those two staring at you,' whispered Tanya. 'It looks as if they're coming over. . .'

And at that point I heard Russian spoken behind me.

'My colleague from New Zealand and I are journalists. I'm from the Soviet Press Agency and I'm escorting our guest. Our guest is interested in you. He saw you were wearing the badge of the Journalists' Union and medal tabs, and he would very much like you to answer some questions.'

'Please do. Come over to our table.' Yevgeni Alexandrovich Pozdnyakov, Soviet Press Agency correspondent, beckoned his colleague over. We introduced ourselves.

'Our guest asks why you have so many decorations and medals. And what are they for?'

'I had to fight the Nazis at one time, and that's what the decorations are for,' I replied. 'And there aren't as many as it appears.'

'You were a journalist during the war?'

'No, I was a sniper at the front. It was near Leningrad, during the blockade.'

'Would you be able to relate a few episodes of battle from your life at the front?' asked Yevgeni Alexandrovich as he translated yet another question from the foreign visitor.

'I'll try.'

The foreign visitor listened with great attention, sometimes interrupting, asking a question of his own and listening further.

We talked like this for probably about an hour. The visitor bowed, thanked me warmly and squeezed my hand for a long time.

The next day we bade farewell to the sea and arrived at the airport. It was still early and there was still plenty of time before our plane took off.

And suddenly I heard:

'Oh, Mister Nikolaev! Good morning'

Looking round, I saw our two acquaintances from yesterday at the Pearl Hotel.

'My colleague was upset that he didn't have his camera with him. He has it with him today and he'd like to photograph you as a memento,' said Yevgeni Alexandrovich.

A while time later I received a letter from my former regimental commissar Ivan Ilyich Agashin in Leningrad.

'Why aren't you writing anything about yourself? One has to find out from New Zealand journalists where you are and what's happened to you ...' Agashin wrote that, as a participant in the Civil War and the Great War for the Fatherland, he was asked to meet a journalist from New Zealand, who had come to Leningrad. While talking about the siege of Leningrad, Agashin mentioned the snipers' movement and my name.

'I met Mr. Yevgeni Nikolaev in Sochi,' said the journalist.

It happens ...

Several months later I received a parcel from Moscow. Inside was a letter, two clippings from a foreign newspaper, and two photos.

> Dear Yevgeni Adrianovich! I am sending you two articles published in the *New Zealand Herald* following conversations with you in Sochi. The two photos will remind you of it. Thank you for your fraternal assistance. With best wishes, Yevgeni Pozdnyakov.

The articles were translated for me. One of them was entitled 'Russian's amazing story', in which he outlined our conversation in Sochi. Everything was correct, with no distortions or fabrications.

The second article was devoted to Agashin and the amazing coincidence that we knew each other.

Well, I would have to fulfil my promise and send my own book to New Zealand as soon as it came out. Let them know there how we defended Leningrad against the Nazis, how we withstood the 900 days of the blockade, and what effort and sacrifices it cost us. May they too fight for peace throughout the whole world ...

# THE
# THIRD✠REICH
## IN 100 OBJECTS
### A MATERIAL HISTORY OF NAZI GERMANY

ROGER MOORHOUSE

FOREWORD BY
RICHARD OVERY

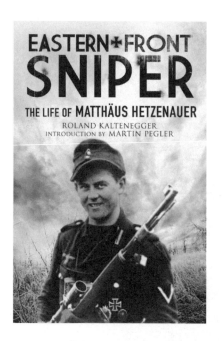

# EASTERN★FRONT SNIPER

## THE LIFE OF MATTHÄUS HETZENAUER

ROLAND KALTENEGGER
INTRODUCTION BY MARTIN PEGLER

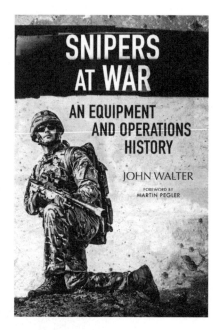

# SNIPERS AT WAR

## AN EQUIPMENT AND OPERATIONS HISTORY

JOHN WALTER

FOREWORD BY
MARTIN PEGLER

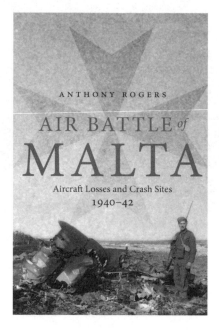

ANTHONY ROGERS

# AIR BATTLE *of*

# MALTA

Aircraft Losses and Crash Sites
1940–42